Ninja Air Fryer Cookbook UK

365 Delicious, Quick & Easy Air Fryer Recipes incl. Side Dishes, Desserts, Snacks and More for Beginners and Advanced Users.

Thomas Schirmer

Copyright © 2023 by   All rights reserved.

The content contained within this book may not be reproduced, duplicated, or transmitted without direct written permission from the author or the publisher. Under no circumstances will any blame or legal responsibility be held against the publisher, or author, for any damages, reparation, or monetary loss due to the information contained within this book, either directly or indirectly.

Legal Notice: This book is copyright protected. It is only for personal use. You cannot amend, distribute, sell, use, quote or paraphrase any part, or the content within this book, without the consent of the author or publisher.

Disclaimer Notice: Please note the information contained within this document is for educational and entertainment purposes only. All effort has been executed to present accurate, up to date, reliable, complete information. No warranties of any kind are declared or implied. Readers acknowledge that the author is not engaged in the rendering of legal, financial, medical, or professional advice. The content within this book has been derived from various sources. Please consult a licensed professional before attempting any techniques outlined in this book. By reading this document, the reader agrees that under no circumstances is the author responsible for any losses, direct or indirect, that are incurred as a result of the use of the information contained within this document, including, but not limited to, errors, omissions, or inaccuracies.

Table of Contents

Table of Contents 3
Chapter 1: Introduction 7
How the Ninja Air Fryer Works 7   The Advantages of the Ninja Air Fryers 8
Foods to Cook in the Ninja Air Fryers 8   Tips and Tricks for Using the Ninja Air Fryers 9

Chapter 2: Measurement Conversions 10
BASIC KITCHEN CONVERSIONS & EQUIVALENTS 10

Chapter 3: Vegetable Side Dishes Recipes 11
Smashed Fried Baby Potatoes 12   Blistered Tomatoes 15
Roasted Brussels Sprouts With Bacon 12   Bacon-jalapeño Cheesy "breadsticks" 15
Asparagus Fries 12   Pancetta Mushroom & Onion Sautée 16
Asparagus Wrapped In Pancetta 12   Hot Okra Wedges 16
Green Peas With Mint 12   Perfect Broccoli 16
Roasted Garlic 13   Mini Hasselback Potatoes 16
Green Beans 13   Twice-baked Potatoes With Pancetta 16
Fried Mashed Potato Balls 13   Cheesy Garlic Bread 17
Foil Packet Lemon Butter Asparagus 13   Crispy Herbed Potatoes 17
Baked Jalapeño And Cheese Cauliflower Mash ... 13   Brussels Sprouts 17
Dauphinoise (potatoes Au Gratin) 14   Cheesy Baked Asparagus 17
Perfect French Fries 14   Buttermilk Biscuits 17
Polenta 14   Buttered Brussels Sprouts 18
Simple Roasted Sweet Potatoes 14   Taco Okra 18
Roasted Rhubarb 14   Spicy Fried Green Beans 18
Roasted Fennel Salad 14   Roasted Garlic And Thyme Tomatoes 18
Sea Salt Radishes 15   Tasty Brussels Sprouts With Guanciale 18
Mouth-watering Provençal Mushrooms 15   Spicy Corn Fritters 19
Easy Parmesan Asparagus 15   Caraway Seed Pretzel Sticks 19
Bacon-wrapped Asparagus 15   Flatbread Dippers 19

Chapter 4: Appetizers And Snacks 20
Honey Tater Tots With Bacon 21   Okra Chips 23
Pickled Chips 21   Cauliflower Buns 24
Garlic Breadsticks 21   Lemon Tofu Cubes 24
Basil Pork Bites 21   Thyme Sweet Potato Chips 24
Home-style Taro Chips 21   Root Vegetable Crisps 24
Rumaki 21   Sweet Apple Fries 24
Roasted Peppers 22   Za'atar Garbanzo Beans 25
Grilled Cheese Sandwich Deluxe 22   Mexican Muffins 25
Cinnamon Apple Crisps 22   Cheesy Tortellini Bites 25
Cheddar Cheese Lumpia Rolls 22   Roasted Chickpeas 25
Fried Goat Cheese 22   Eggs In Avocado Halves 25
Bacon & Blue Cheese Tartlets 23   Bacon-wrapped Cabbage Bites 26
Bacon-wrapped Jalapeño Poppers 23   Amazing Blooming Onion 26
Veggie Chips 23   Bacon-wrapped Goat Cheese Poppers 26
Apple Rollups 23   Fried Ranch Pickles 26

Chapter 5: Bread And Breakfast 27
Black's Bangin' Casserole 28   Egg In A Hole 28
Crispy Bacon 28   Chocolate-hazelnut Bear Claws 29
Tuna And Arugula Salad 28   Chocolate Chip Scones 29
Cinnamon Rolls 28   Spinach-bacon Rollups 29
Very Berry Breakfast Puffs 28   Blueberry Scones 29

Ninja Air Fryer Cookbook

Onion Marinated Skirt Steak 29	Cheesy Cauliflower "hash Browns" 35
Mediterranean Egg Sandwich 30	Spinach Spread 35
Meaty Omelet 30	Smoked Salmon Croissant Sandwich 35
Bacon Eggs 30	Egg White Frittata 35
Cheese Pie 30	Strawberry Pastry 35
Oregano And Coconut Scramble 30	Cinnamon Granola 36
Bacon And Cheese Quiche 30	Eggplant Parmesan Subs 36
Bagels 31	Jalapeño And Bacon Breakfast Pizza 36
Blueberry Muffins 31	Buttery Scallops 36
Breakfast Chimichangas 31	Cream Cheese Danish 36
Chocolate Chip Muffins 31	Easy Egg Bites 37
Fry Bread 31	Mini Tomato Quiche 37
Green Scramble 32	Banana Baked Oatmeal 37
Chives Omelet 32	Zucchini And Spring Onions Cakes 37
Hole In One 32	Egg White Cups 37
Egg Muffins 32	Roasted Golden Mini Potatoes 37
Mini Bacon Egg Quiches 32	Parmesan Garlic Naan 38
Perfect Burgers 33	Breakfast Quiche 38
Thai Turkey Sausage Patties 33	Bacon, Egg, And Cheese Calzones 38
Bacon Puff Pastry Pinwheels 33	Sweet Potato-cinnamon Toast 38
Creamy Parsley Soufflé 33	Grilled Steak With Parsley Salad 38
Jalapeño Egg Cups 33	Pancake For Two 39
Simple Egg Soufflé 34	Inside-out Cheeseburgers 39
Medium Rare Simple Salt And Pepper Steak 34	White Wheat Walnut Bread 39
Grilled Bbq Sausages 34	Pizza Eggs 39
Bunless Breakfast Turkey Burgers 34	Banana-nut Muffins 39
Pigs In A Blanket 34	All-in-one Breakfast Toast 40
Parsley Omelet 34	

Chapter 6: Vegetarians Recipes *41*

Caprese Eggplant Stacks 42	Sweet Pepper Nachos 46
Spinach Pesto Flatbread 42	Healthy Apple-licious Chips 46
Pizza Dough 42	Caramelized Brussels Sprout 46
Tortilla Pizza Margherita 42	Spicy Roasted Cashew Nuts 46
Pesto Vegetable Kebabs 42	Pepper-pineapple With Butter-sugar Glaze 46
Italian Seasoned Easy Pasta Chips 42	Stuffed Portobellos 46
White Cheddar And Mushroom Soufflés 43	Easy Baked Root Veggies 47
Cauliflower Rice–stuffed Peppers 43	Eggplant Parmesan 47
Zucchini Gratin 43	Roasted Vegetable Pita Pizza 47
Cauliflower Pizza Crust 43	Zucchini Topped With Coconut Cream 'n Bacon 47
Spinach And Artichoke–stuffed Peppers 43	Mediterranean Pan Pizza 48
Crispy Cabbage Steaks 44	Two-cheese Grilled Sandwiches 48
Crispy Shawarma Broccoli 44	Turmeric Crispy Chickpeas 48
Buttered Broccoli 44	Cauliflower Steaks Gratin 48
Garlic Okra Chips 44	Spinach And Feta Pinwheels 48
Easy Glazed Carrots 44	Cheese And Bean Enchiladas 49
Crispy Wings With Lemony Old Bay Spice 44	Wine Infused Mushrooms 49
Sweet And Sour Brussel Sprouts 45	Twice-baked Broccoli-cheddar Potatoes 49
Thyme Lentil Patties 45	Basil Tomatoes 49
Tacos 45	Lemon Caper Cauliflower Steaks 49
Breadcrumbs Stuffed Mushrooms 45	Crispy Eggplant Rounds 50
Sweet And Spicy Barbecue Tofu 45	Curried Eggplant 50
Sautéed Spinach 46	

Chapter 7: Fish And Seafood Recipes *51*

Timeless Garlic-lemon Scallops 52	Crunchy Coconut Shrimp 52
Lobster Tails 52	Maple Butter Salmon 52
Almond Topped Trout 52	Tilapia Fish Fillets 53
Sesame Tuna Steak 52	Southern-style Catfish 53

Snow Crab Legs 53
Fish Fillet Sandwich 53
Cajun Flounder Fillets 53
Air Fried Calamari 53
Panko-breaded Cod Fillets 54
Cod Nuggets 54
Cajun Lobster Tails 54
Tilapia Teriyaki 54
Spicy Fish Taco Bowl 54
Thyme Scallops 55
Lemon Pepper–breaded Tilapia 55
Lemon Butter–dill Salmon 55
Flounder Fillets 55
Chili-lime Shrimp 55
Lemon Shrimp And Zucchinis 55
Fish Sticks 56
Herbed Haddock 56
Horseradish-crusted Salmon Fillets 56
Outrageous Crispy Fried Salmon Skin 56
Catfish Nuggets 56
Miso-rubbed Salmon Fillets 57
Italian Baked Cod 57
Lemon-roasted Salmon Fillets 57
Beer-battered Cod 57
Tuna-stuffed Tomatoes 58
Salmon Patties 58
Cajun Salmon 58
Crunchy And Buttery Cod With Ritz Cracker Crust 58
Tortilla-crusted With Lemon Filets 58
Shrimp Al Pesto 58
Ahi Tuna Steaks 59
Easy Lobster Tail With Salted Butetr 59
Crab-stuffed Avocado Boats 59
Potato-wrapped Salmon Fillets 59
Zesty Mahi Mahi 59
Simple Salmon Fillets 59
Sweet Potato–wrapped Shrimp 60
Garlic And Dill Salmon 60
Catalan Sardines With Romesco Sauce 60
Lime Bay Scallops 60
Simple Salmon 60
Easy-peasy Shrimp 60

Chapter 8: Poultry Recipes *61*

Pecan-crusted Chicken Tenders 62
Garlic Parmesan Drumsticks 62
Crispy "fried" Chicken 62
Spinach And Feta Stuffed Chicken Breasts 62
Hasselback Alfredo Chicken 63
Herb-marinated Chicken 63
Fried Herbed Chicken Wings 63
Basic Chicken Breasts 63
Chicken Sausage In Dijon Sauce 63
Garlic Dill Wings 63
Stuffed Chicken 64
Italian Chicken Thighs 64
Lemon Pepper Chicken Wings 64
Paprika Duck 64
Chicken Wrapped In Bacon 64
Chicken Wings 64
Celery Chicken Mix 65
Chicken Fajita Poppers 65
Spinach 'n Bacon Egg Cups 65
Peppery Lemon-chicken Breast 65
Bacon Chicken Mix 65
Chicken Parmesan Casserole 65
Crispy Italian Chicken Thighs 65
Chicken Nuggets 66
Yummy Shredded Chicken 66
Salt And Pepper Wings 66
Yummy Stuffed Chicken Breast 66
Barbecue Chicken Enchiladas 66
Garlic Ginger Chicken 66
Dill Pickle–ranch Wings 67
Italian Roasted Chicken Thighs 67
Buffalo Chicken Meatballs 67
Blackened Chicken Tenders 67
Quick 'n Easy Garlic Herb Wings 67
Teriyaki Chicken Kebabs 67
Easy & Crispy Chicken Wings 68
Rosemary Partridge 68
Buttermilk-fried Chicken Thighs 68
Spice-rubbed Chicken Thighs 68
Party Buffalo Chicken Drumettes 68
Breaded Chicken Patties 69
15-minute Chicken 69
Zesty Ranch Chicken Drumsticks 69
Crispy 'n Salted Chicken Meatballs 69
Sticky Drumsticks 69

Chapter 9: Beef, pork & Lamb Recipes *70*

Peppered Steak Bites 71
Wasabi-coated Pork Loin Chops 71
Egg Stuffed Pork Meatballs 71
Brown Sugar Mustard Pork Loin 71
Rib Eye Steak 71
Mexican-style Shredded Beef 72
Quick & Easy Meatballs 72
Air Fried Thyme Garlic Lamb Chops 72
Bacon And Blue Cheese Burgers 72
Honey Mesquite Pork Chops 72
Parmesan-crusted Pork Chops 73
Sweet And Spicy Spare Ribs 73
Garlic Fillets 73
Lemon-butter Veal Cutlets 73
Flatiron Steak Grill On Parsley Salad 73
Spice-rubbed Pork Loin 74
Mustard Herb Pork Tenderloin 74
Mozzarella-stuffed Meatloaf 74
Pork Belly Marinated In Onion-coconut Cream 74
Easy & The Traditional Beef Roast Recipe 74
Steak Fingers 74
Barbecue Country-style Pork Ribs 75

Empanadas 75	Rosemary Lamb Chops 79
Crispy Smoked Pork Chops 75	Mccornick Pork Chops 79
Sweet And Spicy Pork Ribs 75	Crispy Ham And Eggs 79
Cheddar Bacon Ranch Pinwheels 76	Air Fried Grilled Steak 79
Bacon And Cheese–stuffed Pork Chops 76	Pesto-rubbed Veal Chops 79
Venison Backstrap 76	Steak Bites And Spicy Dipping Sauce 80
Easy-peasy Beef Sliders 76	Simple Lamb Chops 80
Salted 'n Peppered Scored Beef Chuck 76	Lamb Chops 80
Orange And Brown Sugar–glazed Ham 77	Mustard Pork 80
Smokehouse-style Beef Ribs 77	London Broil 80
Fajita Flank Steak Rolls 77	Greek Pork Chops 80
Stuffed Peppers 77	Garlic And Oregano Lamb Chops 81
Pork Chops 77	Roast Beef 81
Spinach And Provolone Steak Rolls 78	Pork Spare Ribs 81
Rib Eye Steak Seasoned With Italian Herb 78	Spinach And Mushroom Steak Rolls 81
Quick & Simple Bratwurst With Vegetables 78	Marinated Steak Kebabs 82
Boneless Ribeyes 78	Blackened Steak Nuggets 82
Steakhouse Filets Mignons 78	Chicken Fried Steak 82
Maple'n Soy Marinated Beef 79	Lamb Burgers 82

Chapter 10: Desserts And Sweets 83

Cocoa Bombs 84	Marshmallow Pastries 87
Cinnamon-sugar Pretzel Bites 84	Nutty Fudge Muffins 87
Orange Marmalade 84	Chocolate Chip Cookie Cake 87
Strawberry Shortcake 84	Easy Keto Danish 87
Cinnamon Pretzels 84	Glazed Donuts 88
Crème Brulee 85	Tortilla Fried Pies 88
Apple Pie 85	Banana Chips With Chocolate Glaze 88
Custard 85	Baked Apple 88
Fiesta Pastries 85	Hearty Banana Pastry 88
Hot Coconut 'n Cocoa Buns 85	Brown Sugar Cookies 88
S'mores Pockets 85	Cinnamon Canned Biscuit Donuts 89
Molten Lava Cakes 86	Fried Banana S'mores 89
Banana And Rice Pudding 86	Fried Pineapple Chunks 89
Kiwi Pastry Bites 86	Pineapple Sticks 89
Oreo-coated Peanut Butter Cups 86	Nutella And Banana Pastries 89

Recipes Index 90

Chapter 1: Introduction

This appliance is aimed at people who want to enjoy tasty, healthy but low-fat food with a crispy texture.

The Ninja Air Fryer is a wonderful piece of kitchen equipment! It literally fries foods using hot dry air—not oil—that circulates around each piece, sealing in the flavor and creating a crust with a fabulous crunch. Yes, crunch.

While an Ninja air fryer may seem like a specialized kitchen appliance, it's not one that will sit and gather dust in your pantry. In addition to creating healthy "fried" foods, you can also bake, grill, roast, steam, and stir-fry using this delightful invention. In fact, you likely will use it every day.

With this appliance you can re-create and enjoy those deep-fried foods you may have given up—donuts, French fries, fried chicken—and take this concept a step further. If you want to cook foods that are not just better for you than deep-fried foods, but also actually healthy, good-for-you foods in and of themselves, this book can help you do just that.

I have always loved fried foods. Growing up, for our birthday dinners, we were allowed to choose our favorite meal. Mine was grilled steak served with homemade French fries that were (gulp) fried in an entire can of solid shortening. That is not a meal I choose today, but, using the air fryer, I can have similar foods that taste even better and that are actually good for me!

When I first ventured into cooking healthy foods in the Ninja air fryer, I was committed to learning to cook food

with less fat and better nutrition. Like you, I'm sure, I also wanted it to taste good and be quick and easy. I love to try new appliances, and this sounded simple. However, I admit I was slightly skeptical at first—Could I possibly create a donut hole that was healthy yet still yummy? Yes—the answer is yes. And the most surprising thing of all? Foods cooked with just hot air can be as crisp and flavorful as those cooked in fat. What's not to love?

You can create different dishes for any occasion or picnic. The Ninja Air Fryer has many useful cooking functions such as maximum crispiness, air frying, grilling, reheating, dehydrating and baking. All the valuable functions are present in one appliance. You don't need to buy a separate appliance for baking or dehydrating food. You can bake chicken, roast beef and grill fish with this appliance. Bake cakes, muffins, cupcakes and pancakes with the baking cooking function.

This Ninja Air Fryer Cookbook UK will introduce you to the features and benefits of this revolutionary appliance. In addition to this, the features of the Ninja Air Fryer are discussed in this cookbook to help you unlock its full potential. Of course, I will also introduce you to 365 simple recipes so that you can use it every day. The Ninja Air Fryer is fairly simple to use. Once you get to know the Ninja Air Fryer, you won't hesitate to prepare delicious meals for your family and friends. Cook your food in the Ninja Air Fryer!

How the Ninja Air Fryer Works

Developed in 2008 in England, a country famous for its fish and chips, the air fryer is a stand-alone appliance that cooks, bakes, fries, grills, and steams food to tender perfection. This heavy-duty appliance was embraced soon after in the United States for its quick cooking ability and versatility.

The air fryer consists of a heating element, a frying basket attached to a pan that catches the juices and fat released as the food cooks, and a fan that pushes hot air around the food. The heating element browns and crisps the exterior while cooking the interior to a safe final temperature. Air-fried ovens cook food at high temperatures with high-pressure air conditioners, while deep-fried cookers cook food in hot oil pans up to a certain temperature. They both cook the food quickly, but the air fryer pan requires about a little time before the cooking for preheating while the deep-frying pan can take more than 10 minutes. Air fries also require little or no oil and deep fries need more oil for cooking the food. The food comes out crispy and delicious in both electrical outlets, but it does not taste the same, usually because deep fried foods are covered with a lot of oil. Some foods need to be deep fried in oil by using a conventional fryer to make it colorful and crispy, while the air fryer needs very little oil to cook food. The hot air technology used in the air fryer makes the air fryer an ideal cooking appliance to cook crispy, tasty, and healthy food within few minutes and without the usage of extra oil.

Ninja Air Fryer Cookbook

There are two kinds of cooking methods: dry heat, such as frying; and wet heat, such as steaming or braising. Surprisingly, cooking food in oil is considered a dry-heat cooking method. The air fryer takes this method one step further by eliminating the oil altogether.

Foods to Cook in the Ninja Air Fryers

Ninja Air fries are fast, and once you understand how they work; they can be used to heat frozen foods or to cook all kinds of fresh foods like chicken, beef, pork, salmon and vegetables. Most meats do not need extra oil because they already have a lot of fat: just add salt and herbs and your favorite spices. Make sure the steaks are rubbed with dry or wet spices- a little moisture leads to delicious results. If you want to bake meat with sauce or honey, wait until the last few minutes of cooking.

Grease the lean chicken breasts and pork chops with a little oil before seasoning. Vegetable oil or canola oil is often recommended for its high smoke content, which means that it can withstand high temperatures in the air fryer.

Vegetables also need to be sprayed with a little oil before frying in the air fryer. We recommend that you sprinkle them with salt before frying in air fryer for proper cooking.

You can cook any kind of food in the air fryer. You can bake, roast, fry, toast, or even crispy any kind of food by using your Ninja air fryer. Once you state using the air fryer, you will forget all other conventional and market available fryers and ovens.

The Advantages of the Ninja Air Fryers

There are various health benefits that the air fryer can provide to you.

1.   Healthy Fried Foods

The air fryers are a healthy option to cook food because they do not need a lot of amount of oil to cook food. There is almost zero percent requirement of the oil to be used for cooking any type of food items. You just need to spray the air fryer basket with any healthy cooking oil. In some cases, you do not need to even spray the air fryer basket. The less consumption of oil or any kind of fat, makes the air fryer a healthy option to cook extremely delicious, crispy, and healthy food.

2.   Uses Less Energy

With the cost of electricity forever climbing, it makes sense to use a kitchen appliance that uses less than your oven or stove. Only a small space is being heated, and the cooking times are faster. The high temperatures, combined with the fan, reduce your cooking time.

3.   Less Mess

Only the basket you cook your food in needs to be cleaned. Your stove and countertops are spared the oil splatter.

4.   Portable

Even the bigger air fryers are small enough for you to take with you when you go on a self-catering vacation.

5.   Easy to Use

No big, clumsy oven trays, or complicated settings.

6.   Convenient Meals for One or Two People

Cooking for yourself can be a bit of a drag. Even cooking for two can feel like a waste of time. When your time spent in the kitchen preparing meals is cut down, and the food you serve is delicious, it is no longer a chore to cook for just one or two people.

7.   Quick Meals for Kids

Hungry kids are grumpy kids. Your air fryer means that your children can enjoy the foods they love best, in almost no time at all.

8.   Perfect Portions

When you cook in a large oven, or you are heating up a lot of oil, you may feel like you need to fill the space with whatever you are cooking. How often do you have leftovers? Due to the smaller size, it is easier to cook just the right amount, without worrying about all the wasted

space.

8   *Ninja Air Fryer Cookbook*

Tips and Tricks for Using the Ninja Air Fryers

Air fryers can give you crispier foods that satisfy your cravings. Here are some great tips for you to get the most out of your air fryer!

1. Shake it!
Be sure to open the fryer and shake what you are cooking around as they "fry" in the basket. Smaller foods such as French fries and chips may compress. Even if a recipe does not mention to rotate, shake, or flip, for the best results, make sure to do so every 5-10 minutes.

2. Do not overcrowd.
Make sure you give foods lots of space for the hot air to circulate effectively around what you are cooking. This will give you the crispy results you crave! Also, it is best to work in small batches.

3. Spray foods.
Most recipes will tell you to do such, but if not, it is a good idea to lightly spray foods with a bit of oil, so they do not stick to the basket as they cook. I suggest investing in a kitchen spray bottle to put oil in. Much easier to spray foods, so you don't totally saturate them with this greasy stuff.

4. Keep dry.
Make sure you pat foods dry before adding them to air fryer basket. This helps to prevent splattering and excess smoking. So, let marinated foods drip a bit before adding and make sure to empty the fat from the bottom of the fryer when you are done cooking foods that are high in fat content.

5. Master other methods of cooking.
The air fryer is not just for frying! It is great for other methods of cooking, such as grilling, roasting, and even baking! It is my go-to appliance to get the best-tasting salmon!

6. Add water when cooking fatty foods.
Add water to the drawer underneath the basket will help to prevent the grease in fattier foods from becoming too hot and causing smoke to engulf your kitchen. Do this with burgers, sausage, and bacon especially.

7. Hold foods down with toothpicks.
On occasion, your air fryer will pick up foods that are light and blow them around the fryer. Secure foods you cook with toothpicks!

8. Open as often as you like.
One of the best benefits of cooking with an air fryer is that you do not have to worry about how often you open it up to check for doneness. If you are an anxious chef, this can give you peace of mind to create yummy meals and snacks every single time!

9. Take out basket before removing food.
If you go to invert the air fryer basket when it is still locked tightly in the drawer, you will dump all the fat that has rendered from your food.

10. Clean the drawer after each use.
The air fryer drawer is extremely easy to clean and quite hassle-free. But if you leave it unwashed, you can risk contaminating future food you cook, and you may have a nasty smell takeover your kitchen. Simply clean it after every use to prevent this.

11. Use the air dryer to dry the appliance out.
After you wash the basket and air fryer drawer, you can pop them back into the fryer and turn on the appliance for 2-3 minutes. This is a great way to thoroughly dry it for your next use!

Chapter 2: Measurement Conversions

BASIC KITCHEN CONVERSIONS & EQUIVALENTS

DRY MEASUREMENTS CONVERSION CHART
3 TEASPOONS = 1 TABLESPOON = 1/16 CUP
6 TEASPOONS = 2 TABLESPOONS = 1/8 CUP
12 TEASPOONS = 4 TABLESPOONS = 1/4 CUP
24 TEASPOONS = 8 TABLESPOONS = 1/2 CUP
36 TEASPOONS = 12 TABLESPOONS = 3/4 CUP
48 TEASPOONS = 16 TABLESPOONS = 1 CUP

METRIC TO US COOKING CONVERSIONS
OVEN TEMPERATURES
120 °C = 250 °F
160 °C = 320 °F
180° C = 360 °F
205 °C = 400 °F
220 °C = 425 °F

LIQUID MEASUREMENTS CONVERSION CHART
8 FLUID OUNCES = 1 CUP = 1/2 PINT = 1/4 QUART
16 FLUID OUNCES = 2 CUPS = 1 PINT = 1/2 QUART
32 FLUID OUNCES = 4 CUPS = 2 PINTS = 1 QUART = 1/4 GALLON
128 FLUID OUNCES = 16 CUPS = 8 PINTS = 4 QUARTS
= 1 GALLON

BAKING IN GRAMS
1 CUP FLOUR = 140 GRAMS
1 CUP SUGAR = 150 GRAMS
1 CUP POWDERED SUGAR = 160 GRAMS
1 CUP HEAVY CREAM = 235 GRAMS

VOLUME
1 MILLILITER = 1/5 TEASPOON
5 ML = 1 TEASPOON
15 ML = 1 TABLESPOON
240 ML = 1 CUP OR 8 FLUID OUNCES
1 LITER = 34 FL. OUNCES

WEIGHT
1 GRAM = .035 OUNCES
100 GRAMS = 3.5 OUNCES
500 GRAMS = 1.1 POUNDS
1 KILOGRAM = 35 OUNCES

US TO METRIC COOKING CONVERSIONS
1/5 TSP = 1 ML
1 TSP = 5 ML
1 TBSP = 15 ML
1 FL OUNCE = 30 ML
1 CUP = 237 ML
1 PINT (2 CUPS) = 473 ML
1 QUART (4 CUPS) = .95 LITER
1 GALLON (16 CUPS) = 3.8 LITERS
1 OZ = 28 GRAMS
1 POUND = 454 GRAMS

BUTTER
1 CUP BUTTER = 2 STICKS = 8 OUNCES = 230 GRAMS = 8 TABLESPOONS

WHAT DOES 1 CUP EQUAL
1 CUP = 8 FLUID OUNCES
1 CUP = 16 TABLESPOONS
1 CUP = 48 TEASPOONS
1 CUP = 1/2 PINT
1 CUP = 1/4 QUART
1 CUP = 1/16 GALLON
1 CUP = 240 ML

BAKING PAN CONVERSIONS
1 CUP ALL-PURPOSE FLOUR = 4.5 OZ
1 CUP ROLLED OATS = 3 OZ 1 LARGE EGG = 1.7 OZ
1 CUP BUTTER = 8 OZ 1 CUP MILK = 8 OZ
1 CUP HEAVY CREAM = 8.4 OZ
1 CUP GRANULATED SUGAR = 7.1 OZ
1 CUP PACKED BROWN SUGAR = 7.75 OZ
1 CUP VEGETABLE OIL = 7.7 OZ
1 CUP UNSIFTED POWDERED SUGAR = 4.4 OZ

BAKING PAN CONVERSIONS
9-INCH ROUND CAKE PAN = 12 CUPS
10-INCH TUBE PAN =16 CUPS
11-INCH BUNDT PAN = 12 CUPS
9-INCH SPRINGFORM PAN = 10 CUPS
9 X 5 INCH LOAF PAN = 8 CUPS
9-INCH SQUARE PAN = 8 CUPS

Chapter 3: Vegetable Side Dishes Recipes

Smashed Fried Baby Potatoes

Servings: 3
Cooking Time: 18 Minutes
Ingredients:
- 1½ pounds baby red or baby Yukon gold potatoes
- ¼ cup butter, melted
- 1 teaspoon olive oil
- ½ teaspoon paprika
- 1 teaspoon dried parsley
- salt and freshly ground black pepper
- 2 scallions, finely chopped

Directions:
1. Bring a large pot of salted water to a boil. Add the potatoes and boil for 18 minutes or until the potatoes are fork-tender.
2. Drain the potatoes and transfer them to a cutting board to cool slightly. Spray or brush the bottom of a drinking glass with a little oil. Smash or flatten the potatoes by pressing the glass down on each potato slowly. Try not to completely flatten the potato or smash it so hard that it breaks apart.
3. Combine the melted butter, olive oil, paprika, and parsley together.
4. Preheat the air fryer to 400°F (205°C).
5. Spray the bottom of the air fryer basket with oil and transfer one layer of the smashed potatoes into the basket. Brush with some of the butter mixture and season generously with salt and freshly ground black pepper.
6. Air-fry at 400°F (205°C) for 10 minutes. Carefully flip the potatoes over and air-fry for an additional 8 minutes until crispy and lightly browned.
7. Keep the potatoes warm in a 170°F (75°C) oven or tent with aluminum foil while you cook the second batch. Sprinkle minced scallions over the potatoes and serve warm.

Roasted Brussels Sprouts With Bacon

Servings: 4
Cooking Time: 20 Minutes
Ingredients:
- 4 slices thick-cut bacon, chopped (about ¼ pound)
- 1 pound Brussels sprouts, halved (or quartered if large)
- freshly ground black pepper

Directions:
1. Preheat the air fryer to 380°F (195°C).
2. Air-fry the bacon for 5 minutes, shaking the basket once or twice during the cooking time.
3. Add the Brussels sprouts to the basket and drizzle a little bacon fat from the bottom of the air fryer drawer into the basket. Toss the sprouts to coat with the bacon fat. Air-fry for an additional 15 minutes, or until the Brussels sprouts are tender to a knifepoint.
4. Season with freshly ground black pepper.

Asparagus Fries

Servings: 4
Cooking Time: 5 Minutes Per Batch
Ingredients:
- 12 ounces fresh asparagus spears with tough ends trimmed off
- 2 egg whites
- ¼ cup water
- ¾ cup panko breadcrumbs
- ¼ cup grated Parmesan cheese, plus 2 tablespoons
- ¼ teaspoon salt
- oil for misting or cooking spray

Directions:
1. Preheat air fryer to 390°F (200°C).
2. In a shallow dish, beat egg whites and water until slightly foamy.
3. In another shallow dish, combine panko, Parmesan, and salt.
4. Dip asparagus spears in egg, then roll in crumbs. Spray with oil or cooking spray.
5. Place a layer of asparagus in air fryer basket, leaving just a little space in between each spear. Stack another layer on top, crosswise. Cook at 390°F (200°C) for 5 minutes, until crispy and golden brown.
6. Repeat to cook remaining asparagus.

Asparagus Wrapped In Pancetta

Servings: 4
Cooking Time: 30 Minutes
Ingredients:
- 20 asparagus trimmed
- Salt and pepper pepper
- 4 pancetta slices
- 1 tbsp fresh sage, chopped

Directions:
1. Sprinkle the asparagus with fresh sage, salt and pepper. Toss to coat. Make 4 bundles of 5 spears by wrapping the center of the bunch with one slice of pancetta.
2. Preheat air fryer to 400°F (205°C). Put the bundles in the greased frying basket and Air Fry for 8-10 minutes or until the pancetta is brown and the asparagus are starting to char on the edges. Serve immediately.

Green Peas With Mint

Servings: 4
Cooking Time: 5 Minutes
Ingredients:
- 1 cup shredded lettuce
- 1 10-ounce package frozen green peas, thawed
- 1 tablespoon fresh mint, shredded
- 1 teaspoon melted butter

Directions:
1. Lay the shredded lettuce in the air fryer basket.
2. Toss together the peas, mint, and melted butter and spoon over the lettuce.
3. Cook at 360°F (180°C) for 5minutes, until peas are warm and lettuce wilts.

Roasted Garlic

Servings: 20
Cooking Time: 40 Minutes
Ingredients:
- 20 Peeled medium garlic cloves
- 2 tablespoons, plus more Olive oil

Directions:
1. Preheat the air fryer to 400°F (205°C).
2. Set a 10-inch sheet of aluminum foil on your work surface for a small batch, a 14-inch sheet for a medium batch, or a 16-inch sheet for a large batch. Put the garlic cloves in its center in one layer without bunching the cloves together. Drizzle the small batch with 1 tablespoon oil, the medium batch with 2 tablespoons, or the large one with 3 tablespoons. Fold up the sides and seal the foil into a packet.
3. When the machine is at temperature, put the packet in the basket. Air-fry for 40 minutes, or until very fragrant. The cloves inside should be golden and soft.
4. Transfer the packet to a cutting board. Cool for 5 minutes, then open and use the cloves hot. Or cool them to room temperature, set them in a small container or jar, pour in enough olive oil to cover them, seal or cover the container, and refrigerate for up to 2 weeks.

Green Beans

Servings: 4
Cooking Time: 12 Minutes
Ingredients:
- 1 pound fresh green beans
- 2 tablespoons Italian salad dressing
- salt and pepper

Directions:
1. Wash beans and snap off stem ends.
2. In a large bowl, toss beans with Italian dressing.
3. Cook at 330°F (165°C) for 5minutes. Shake basket or stir and cook 5minutes longer. Shake basket again and, if needed, continue cooking for 2 minutes, until as tender as you like. Beans should shrivel slightly and brown in places.
4. Sprinkle with salt and pepper to taste.

Fried Mashed Potato Balls

Servings:4
Cooking Time: 10 Minutes
Ingredients:
- 2 cups mashed potatoes
- ¾ cup sour cream, divided
- 1 teaspoon salt
- ½ teaspoon ground black pepper
- 1 cup shredded sharp Cheddar cheese
- 4 slices bacon, cooked and crumbled
- 1 cup panko bread crumbs
- Cooking spray

Directions:
1. Preheat the air fryer to 400°F (205°C). Cut parchment paper to fit the air fryer basket.
2. In a large bowl, mix mashed potatoes, ½ cup sour cream, salt, pepper, Cheddar, and bacon. Form twelve balls using 2 tablespoons of the potato mixture per ball.
3. Divide remaining ¼ cup sour cream evenly among mashed potato balls, coating each before rolling in bread crumbs.
4. Place balls on parchment in the air fryer basket and spritz with cooking spray. Cook 10 minutes until brown. Serve warm.

Foil Packet Lemon Butter Asparagus

Servings: 4
Cooking Time: 15 Minutes
Ingredients:
- 1 pound asparagus, ends trimmed
- ¼ cup salted butter, cubed
- Zest and juice of ½ medium lemon
- ½ teaspoon salt
- ¼ teaspoon ground black pepper

Directions:
1. Preheat the air fryer to 375°F (190°C). Cut a 6" × 6" square of foil.
2. Place asparagus on foil square.
3. Dot asparagus with butter. Sprinkle lemon zest, salt, and pepper on top of asparagus. Drizzle lemon juice over asparagus.
4. Fold foil over asparagus and seal the edges closed to form a packet.
5. Place in the air fryer basket and cook 15 minutes until tender. Serve warm.

Baked Jalapeño And Cheese Cauliflower Mash

Servings:6
Cooking Time: 15 Minutes
Ingredients:
- 1 steamer bag cauliflower florets, cooked according to package instructions
- 2 tablespoons salted butter, softened
- 2 ounces cream cheese, softened
- ½ cup shredded sharp Cheddar cheese
- ¼ cup pickled jalapeños
- ½ teaspoon salt
- ¼ teaspoon ground black pepper

Directions:
1. Place cooked cauliflower into a food processor with remaining ingredients. Pulse twenty times until cauliflower is smooth and all ingredients are combined.
2. Spoon mash into an ungreased 6" round nonstick baking dish. Place dish into air fryer basket. Adjust the temperature to 380°F (195°C) and set the timer for 15 minutes. The top will be golden brown when done. Serve warm.

Dauphinoise (potatoes Au Gratin)
Servings: 4
Cooking Time: 30 Minutes
Ingredients:
- ½ cup grated cheddar cheese
- 3 peeled potatoes, sliced
- ½ cup milk
- ½ cup heavy cream
- Salt and pepper to taste
- 1 tsp ground nutmeg

Directions:
1. Preheat air fryer to 350°F (175°C). Place the milk, heavy cream, salt, pepper, and nutmeg in a bowl and mix well. Dip in the potato slices and arrange on a baking dish. Spoon the remaining mixture over the potatoes. Scatter the grated cheddar cheese on top. Place the baking dish in the air fryer and Bake for 20 minutes. Serve warm and enjoy!

Perfect French Fries
Servings: 3
Cooking Time: 37 Minutes
Ingredients:
- 1 pound Large russet potato(es)
- Vegetable oil or olive oil spray
- ½ teaspoon Table salt

Directions:
1. Cut each potato lengthwise into ¼-inch-thick slices. Cut each of these lengthwise into ¼-inch-thick matchsticks.
2. Set the potato matchsticks in a big bowl of cool water and soak for 5 minutes. Drain in a colander set in the sink, then spread the matchsticks out on paper towels and dry them very well.
3. Preheat the air fryer to 225°F (105°C).
4. When the machine is at temperature, arrange the matchsticks in an even layer in the basket. Air-fry for 20 minutes, tossing and rearranging the fries twice.
5. Pour the contents of the basket into a big bowl. Increase the air fryer's temperature to 325°F (160°C).
6. Generously coat the fries with vegetable or olive oil spray. Toss well, then coat them again to make sure they're covered on all sides, tossing a couple of times to make sure.
7. When the machine is at temperature, pour the fries into the basket and air-fry for 12 minutes, tossing and rearranging the fries at least twice.
8. Increase the machine's temperature to 375°F (190°C). Air-fry for 5 minutes more, tossing and rearranging the fries at least twice to keep them from burning and to make sure they all get an even measure of the heat, until brown and crisp.
9. Pour the contents of the basket into a serving bowl. Toss the fries with the salt and serve hot.

Polenta
Servings: 4
Cooking Time: 15 Minutes
Ingredients:
- 1 pound polenta
- ¼ cup flour
- oil for misting or cooking spray

Directions:
1. Cut polenta into ½-inch slices.
2. Dip slices in flour to coat well. Spray both sides with oil or cooking spray.
3. Cook at 390°F (200°C) for 5minutes. Turn polenta and spray both sides again with oil.
4. Cook 10 more minutes or until brown and crispy.

Simple Roasted Sweet Potatoes
Servings: 2
Cooking Time: 45 Minutes
Ingredients:
- 2 10- to 12-ounce sweet potato(es)

Directions:
1. Preheat the air fryer to 350°F (175°C).
2. Prick the sweet potato(es) in four or five different places with the tines of a flatware fork.
3. When the machine is at temperature, set the sweet potato(es) in the basket with as much air space between them as possible. Air-fry undisturbed for 45 minutes, or until soft when pricked with a fork.
4. Use kitchen tongs to transfer the sweet potato(es) to a wire rack. Cool for 5 minutes before serving.

Roasted Rhubarb
Servings: 4
Cooking Time: 15 Minutes
Ingredients:
- 1 pound rhubarb, cut in chunks
- 2 teaspoons olive oil
- 2 tablespoons orange zest
- ½ cup walnuts, chopped
- ½ teaspoon sugar

Directions:
1. In your air fryer, mix all the listed ingredients, and toss.
2. Cook at 380ºF for 15 minutes.
3. Divide the rhubarb between plates and serve as a side dish.

Roasted Fennel Salad
Servings: 3
Cooking Time: 20 Minutes
Ingredients:
- 3 cups (about ¾ pound) Trimmed fennel, roughly chopped
- 1½ tablespoons Olive oil
- ¼ teaspoon Table salt
- ¼ teaspoon Ground black pepper
- 1½ tablespoons White balsamic vinegar

Directions:
1. Preheat the air fryer to 400°F (205°C).
2. Toss the fennel, olive oil, salt, and pepper in a large bowl until the fennel is well coated in the oil.

3. When the machine is at temperature, pour the fennel into the basket, spreading it out into as close to one layer as possible. Air-fry for 20 minutes, tossing and rearranging the fennel pieces twice so that any covered or touching parts get exposed to the air currents, until golden at the edges and softened.
4. Pour the fennel into a serving bowl. Add the vinegar while hot. Toss well, then cool a couple of minutes before serving. Or serve at room temperature.

Sea Salt Radishes
Servings: 4
Cooking Time: 25 Minutes
Ingredients:
- 1 lb radishes
- 2 tbsp olive oil
- ½ tsp sea salt
- ½ tsp garlic powder

Directions:
1. Preheat air fryer to 360°F (1800°C). Toss the radishes with olive oil, garlic powder, and salt in a bowl. Pour them into the air fryer. Air Fry for 18 minutes, turning once. Serve.

Mouth-watering Provençal Mushrooms
Servings: 4
Cooking Time: 35 Minutes
Ingredients:
- 2 lb mushrooms, quartered
- 2-3 tbsp olive oil
- ½ tsp garlic powder
- 2 tsp herbs de Provence
- 2 tbsp dry white wine

Directions:
1. Preheat air fryer to 320°F (160°C). Beat together the olive oil, garlic powder, herbs de Provence, and white wine in a bowl. Add the mushrooms and toss gently to coat. Spoon the mixture onto the frying basket and Bake for 16-18 minutes, stirring twice. Serve hot and enjoy!

Easy Parmesan Asparagus
Servings: 4
Cooking Time: 15 Minutes
Ingredients:
- 3 tsp grated Parmesan cheese
- 1 lb asparagus, trimmed
- 2 tsp olive oil
- Salt to taste
- 1 clove garlic, minced
- ½ lemon

Directions:
1. Preheat air fryer at 375ºF. Toss the asparagus and olive oil in a bowl, place them in the frying basket, and Air Fry for 8-10 minutes, tossing once. Transfer them into a large serving dish. Sprinkle with salt, garlic, and Parmesan cheese and toss until coated. Serve immediately with a squeeze of lemon. Enjoy!

Bacon-wrapped Asparagus
Servings: 4
Cooking Time: 10 Minutes
Ingredients:
- 1 tablespoon extra-virgin olive oil
- ½ teaspoon sea salt
- ¼ cup grated Parmesan cheese
- 1 pound asparagus, ends trimmed
- 8 slices bacon

Directions:
1. Preheat the air fryer to 380°F (195°C).
2. In large bowl, mix together the olive oil, sea salt, and Parmesan cheese. Toss the asparagus in the olive oil mixture.
3. Evenly divide the asparagus into 8 bundles. Wrap 1 piece of bacon around each bundle, not overlapping the bacon but spreading it across the bundle.
4. Place the asparagus bundles into the air fryer basket, not touching. Work in batches as needed.
5. Cook for 8 minutes; check for doneness, and cook another 2 minutes.

Blistered Tomatoes
Servings: 20
Cooking Time: 15 Minutes
Ingredients:
- 1½ pounds Cherry or grape tomatoes
- Olive oil spray
- 1½ teaspoons Balsamic vinegar
- ¼ teaspoon Table salt
- ¼ teaspoon Ground black pepper

Directions:
1. Put the basket in a drawer-style air fryer, or a baking tray in the lower third of a toaster oven–style air fryer. Place a 6-inch round cake pan in the basket or on the tray for a small batch, a 7-inch round cake pan for a medium batch, or an 8-inch round cake pan for a large one. Heat the air fryer to 400°F (205°C) with the pan in the basket. When the machine is at temperature, keep heating the pan for 5 minutes more.
2. Place the tomatoes in a large bowl, coat them with the olive oil spray, toss gently, then spritz a couple of times more, tossing after each spritz, until the tomatoes are glistening.
3. Pour the tomatoes into the cake pan and air-fry undisturbed for 10 minutes, or until they split and begin to brown.
4. Use kitchen tongs and a nonstick-safe spatula, or silicone baking mitts, to remove the cake pan from the basket. Toss the hot tomatoes with the vinegar, salt, and pepper. Cool in the pan for a few minutes before serving.

Bacon-jalapeño Cheesy "breadsticks"
Servings:8
Cooking Time: 15 Minutes
Ingredients:
- 2 cups shredded mozzarella cheese
- ¼ cup grated Parmesan cheese

- ¼ cup chopped pickled jalapeños
- 2 large eggs, whisked
- 4 slices cooked sugar-free bacon, chopped

Directions:
1. Mix all ingredients together in a large bowl. Cut a piece of parchment paper to fit inside air fryer basket.
2. Dampen your hands with a bit of water and press out mixture into a circle to fit on ungreased parchment. You may need to separate into two smaller circles, depending on the size of air fryer.
3. Place parchment with cheese mixture into air fryer basket. Adjust the temperature to 320°F (160°C) and set the timer for 15 minutes. Carefully flip when 5 minutes remain on timer. The top will be golden brown when done. Slice into eight sticks. Serve warm.

Pancetta Mushroom & Onion Sautée
Servings:4
Cooking Time: 20 Minutes
Ingredients:
- 16 oz white button mushrooms, stems trimmed, halved
- 1 onion, cut into half-moons
- 4 pancetta slices, diced
- 1 clove garlic, minced

Directions:
1. Preheat air fryer to 350°F. Add all ingredients, except for the garlic, to the frying basket and Air Fry for 8 minutes, tossing once. Stir in the garlic and cook for 1 more minute. Serve right away.

Hot Okra Wedges
Servings: 2
Cooking Time: 35 Minutes
Ingredients:
- 1 cup okra, sliced
- 1 cup breadcrumbs
- 2 eggs, beaten
- A pinch of black pepper
- 1 tsp crushed red peppers
- 2 tsp hot Tabasco sauce

Directions:
1. Preheat air fryer to 350°F (175°C). Place the eggs and Tabasco sauce in a bowl and stir thoroughly; set aside. In a separate mixing bowl, combine the breadcrumbs, crushed red peppers, and pepper. Dip the okra into the beaten eggs, then coat in the crumb mixture. Lay the okra pieces on the greased frying basket. Air Fry for 14-16 minutes, shaking the basket several times during cooking. When ready, the okra will be crispy and golden brown. Serve.

Perfect Broccoli
Servings: 4
Cooking Time: 12 Minutes
Ingredients:
- 5 cups 1- to 1½-inch fresh broccoli florets (not frozen)
- Olive oil spray
- ¾ teaspoon Table salt

1. **Directions:** 19200°C) .
2. Put the broccoli florets in a big bowl, coat them generously with olive oil spray, then toss to coat all surfaces, even down into the crannies, spraying them in a couple of times more. Sprinkle the salt on top and toss again.
3. When the machine is at temperature, pour the florets into the basket. Air-fry for 10 minutes, tossing and rearranging the pieces twice so that all the covered or touching bits are eventually exposed to the air currents, until lightly browned but still crunchy.
4. Pour the florets into a serving bowl. Cool for a minute or two, then serve hot.

Mini Hasselback Potatoes
Servings: 4
Cooking Time: 25 Minutes
Ingredients:
- 1½ pounds baby Yukon Gold potatoes
- 5 tablespoons butter, cut into very thin slices
- salt and freshly ground black pepper
- 1 tablespoon vegetable oil
- ¼ cup grated Parmesan cheese (optional)
- chopped fresh parsley or chives

Directions:
1. Preheat the air fryer to 400°F (205°C).
2. Make six to eight deep vertical slits across the top of each potato about three quarters of the way down. Make sure the slits are deep enough to allow the slices to spread apart a little, but don't cut all the way through the potato. Place a thin slice of butter between each of the slices and season generously with salt and pepper.
3. Transfer the potatoes to the air fryer basket. Pack them in next to each other. It's alright if some of the potatoes sit on top or rest on another potato. Air-fry for 20 minutes.
4. Spray or brush the potatoes with a little vegetable oil and sprinkle the Parmesan cheese on top. Air-fry for an additional 5 minutes. Garnish with chopped parsley or chives and serve hot.

Twice-baked Potatoes With Pancetta
Servings: 5
Cooking Time: 30 Minutes
Ingredients:
- 2 teaspoons canola oil
- 5 large russet potatoes, peeled
- Sea salt and ground black pepper, to taste
- 5 slices pancetta, chopped
- 5 tablespoons Swiss cheese, shredded

Directions:
1. Start by preheating your Air Fryer to 360 °F.
2. Drizzle the canola oil all over the potatoes. Place the potatoes in the Air Fryer basket and cook approximately 20 minutes, shaking the basket periodically.

3. Lightly crush the potatoes to split and season them with salt and ground black pepper. Add the pancetta and cheese.
4. Place in the preheated Air Fryer and bake an additional 5 minutes or until cheese has melted. Bon appétit!

Cheesy Garlic Bread

Servings: 6
Cooking Time: 12 Minutes
Ingredients:
- 1 cup self-rising flour
- 1 cup plain full-fat Greek yogurt
- ¼ cup salted butter, softened
- 1 tablespoon minced garlic
- 1 cup shredded mozzarella cheese

Directions:
1. Preheat the air fryer to 320°F (160°C). Cut parchment paper to fit the air fryer basket.
2. In a large bowl, mix flour and yogurt until a sticky, soft dough forms. Let sit 5 minutes.
3. Turn dough onto a lightly floured surface. Knead dough 1 minute, then transfer to prepared parchment. Press out into an 8" round.
4. In a small bowl, mix butter and garlic. Brush over dough. Sprinkle with mozzarella.
5. Place in the air fryer and cook 12 minutes until edges are golden and cheese is brown. Serve warm.

Crispy Herbed Potatoes

Servings: 6
Cooking Time: 20 Minutes
Ingredients:
- 3 medium baking potatoes, washed and cubed
- ½ teaspoon dried thyme
- 1 teaspoon minced dried rosemary
- ½ teaspoon garlic powder
- 1 teaspoon sea salt
- ½ teaspoon black pepper
- 2 tablespoons extra-virgin olive oil
- ¼ cup chopped parsley

Directions:
1. Preheat the air fryer to 390°F (200°C).
2. Pat the potatoes dry. In a large bowl, mix together the cubed potatoes, thyme, rosemary, garlic powder, sea salt, and pepper. Drizzle and toss with olive oil.
3. Pour the herbed potatoes into the air fryer basket. Cook for 20 minutes, stirring every 5 minutes.
4. Toss the cooked potatoes with chopped parsley and serve immediately.
5. VARY IT! Potatoes are versatile — add any spice or seasoning mixture you prefer and create your own favorite side dish.

Brussels Sprouts

Servings: 3
Cooking Time: 5 Minutes
Ingredients:
- 1 10-ounce package frozen brussels sprouts, thawed and halved
- 2 teaspoons olive oil
- salt and pepper

Directions:
1. Toss the brussels sprouts and olive oil together.
2. Place them in the air fryer basket and season to taste with salt and pepper.
3. Cook at 360°F (180°C) for approximately 5minutes, until the edges begin to brown.

Cheesy Baked Asparagus

Servings:4
Cooking Time: 18 Minutes
Ingredients:
- ½ cup heavy whipping cream
- ½ cup grated Parmesan cheese
- 2 ounces cream cheese, softened
- 1 pound asparagus, ends trimmed, chopped into 1" pieces
- ¼ teaspoon salt
- ¼ teaspoon ground black pepper

Directions:
1. In a medium bowl, whisk together heavy cream, Parmesan, and cream cheese until combined.
2. Place asparagus into an ungreased 6" round nonstick baking dish. Pour cheese mixture over top and sprinkle with salt and pepper.
3. Place dish into air fryer basket. Adjust the temperature to 350°F (175°C) and set the timer for 18 minutes. Asparagus will be tender when done. Serve warm.

Buttermilk Biscuits

Servings: 5
Cooking Time: 14 Minutes
Ingredients:
- 1⅔ cups, plus more for dusting All-purpose flour
- 1½ teaspoons Baking powder
- ¼ teaspoon Table salt
- 3 tablespoons plus 1 teaspoon Butter, cold and cut into small pieces
- ½ cup plus ½ tablespoon Cold buttermilk, regular or low-fat
- 2½ tablespoons Butter, melted and cooled

Directions:
1. Preheat the air fryer to 400°F (205°C).
2. Mix the flour, baking powder, and salt in a large bowl. Use a pastry cutter or a sturdy flatware fork to cut the cold butter pieces into the flour mixture, working the fat through the tines again and again until the mixture resembles coarse dry sand. Stir in the buttermilk to make a dough.
3. Very lightly dust a clean, dry work surface with flour. Turn the dough out onto it, dip your clean hands into flour, and press the dough into a ¾-inch-thick circle. Use a 3-inch round cookie cutter or sturdy drinking glass to cut the dough into rounds. Gather the dough scraps together, lightly shape again into a ¾-inch-thick circle, and cut out a few more rounds. You'll end up with 4 raw biscuits for a small air fryer, 5 for a medium, or 6 for a large.

Ninja Air Fryer Cookbook

4. For a small air fryer, brush the inside of a 6-inch round cake pan with a little more than half of the melted butter, then set the 4 raw biscuits in it, letting them touch but without squishing them.
5. For a medium air fryer, do the same with half of the melted butter in a 7-inch round cake pan and 5 raw biscuits.
6. And for a large air fryer, use a little more than half the melted butter to brush the inside of an 8-inch round cake pan, and set the 6 raw biscuits in it in the same way.
7. Brush the tops of the raw biscuits with the remaining melted butter.
8. Air-fry undisturbed for 14 minutes, or until the biscuits are golden brown and dry to the touch.
9. Using kitchen tongs and a nonstick-safe spatula, two hot pads, or silicone baking mitts, remove the cake pan from the basket and set it on a wire rack. Cool undisturbed for a couple of minutes. Turn the biscuits out onto the wire rack to cool for a couple of minutes more before serving.

Buttered Brussels Sprouts
Servings: 4
Cooking Time: 30 Minutes
Ingredients:
- ¼ cup grated Parmesan
- 2 tbsp butter, melted
- 1 lb Brussels sprouts
- Salt and pepper to taste

Directions:
1. Preheat air fryer to 330°F (165°C). Trim the bottoms of the sprouts and remove any discolored leaves. Place the sprouts in a medium bowl along with butter, salt and pepper. Toss to coat, then place them in the frying basket. Roast for 20 minutes, shaking the basket twice. When done, the sprouts should be crisp with golden-brown color. Plate the sprouts in a serving dish and toss with Parmesan cheese.

Taco Okra
Servings: 3
Cooking Time: 10 Minutes
Ingredients:
- 9 oz okra, chopped
- 1 teaspoon taco seasoning
- 1 teaspoon sunflower oil

Directions:
1. In the mixing bowl mix up chopped okra, taco seasoning, and sunflower oil. Then preheat the air fryer to 385°F. Put the okra mixture in the air fryer and cook it for 5 minutes. Then shake the vegetables well and cook them for 5 minutes more.

Spicy Fried Green Beans
Servings: 2
Cooking Time: 8 Minutes
Ingredients:
- 12 ounces green beans, trimmed
- 2 small dried hot red chili peppers (like árbol)
- ¼ cup panko breadcrumbs
- 1 tablespoon olive oil
- ½ teaspoon salt
- ⅛ teaspoon crushed red pepper flakes
- 2 scallions, thinly sliced

Directions:
1. Preheat the air fryer to 400°F (205°C).
2. Toss the green beans, chili peppers and panko breadcrumbs with the olive oil, salt and crushed red pepper flakes.
3. Air-fry for 8 minutes, shaking the basket once during the cooking process. The crumbs will fall into the bottom drawer – don't worry.
4. Transfer the green beans to a serving dish, sprinkle the scallions and the toasted crumbs from the air fryer drawer on top and serve. The dried peppers are not to be eaten, but they do look nice with the green beans. You can leave them in, or take them out as you please.

Roasted Garlic And Thyme Tomatoes
Servings: 2
Cooking Time: 15 Minutes
Ingredients:
- 4 Roma tomatoes
- 1 tablespoon olive oil
- salt and freshly ground black pepper
- 1 clove garlic, minced
- ½ teaspoon dried thyme

Directions:
1. Preheat the air fryer to 390°F (200°C).
2. Cut the tomatoes in half and scoop out the seeds and any pithy parts with your fingers. Place the tomatoes in a bowl and toss with the olive oil, salt, pepper, garlic and thyme.
3. Transfer the tomatoes to the air fryer, cut side up. Air-fry for 15 minutes. The edges should just start to brown. Let the tomatoes cool to an edible temperature for a few minutes and then use in pastas, on top of crostini, or as an accompaniment to any poultry, meat or fish.

Tasty Brussels Sprouts With Guanciale
Servings: 4
Cooking Time: 50 Minutes
Ingredients:
- 3 guanciale slices, halved
- 1 lb Brussels sprouts, halved
- 2 tbsp olive oil
- ¼ tsp salt
- ¼ tsp dried thyme

Directions:
1. Preheat air fryer to 350°F (175°C). Air Fry Lay the guanciale in the air fryer, until crispy, 10 minutes. Remove and drain on a paper towel. Give the guanciale a rough chop and Set aside. Coat Brussels sprouts with olive oil in a large bowl. Add salt and thyme, then toss. Place the sprouts in the frying basket. Air Fry for about 12-15 minutes, shake the basket once until the sprouts are golden and tender. Top with guanciale and serve.

Spicy Corn Fritters

Servings: 4
Cooking Time: 22 Minutes
Ingredients:
- 1 can yellow corn, drained
- ½ cup all-purpose flour
- ¾ cup shredded pepper jack cheese
- 1 large egg
- ½ teaspoon chili powder
- ¼ teaspoon garlic powder
- ½ teaspoon salt
- ¼ teaspoon ground black pepper

Directions:
1. Cut parchment paper to fit the air fryer basket.
2. In a large bowl, mix all ingredients until well combined. Using a ½-cup scoop, separate mixture into four portions.
3. Gently press each into a 4" round and spritz with cooking spray. Place in freezer 10 minutes.
4. Preheat the air fryer to 400°F (205°C).
5. Place fritters in the air fryer basket and cook 12 minutes, turning halfway through cooking time, until fritters are brown on the top and edges and firm to the touch. Serve warm.

Caraway Seed Pretzel Sticks

Servings: 4
Cooking Time: 30 Minutes
Ingredients:
- ½ pizza dough
- 1 tsp baking soda
- 2 tbsp caraway seeds
- 1 cup of hot water
- Cooking spray

Directions:
1. Preheat air fryer to 400°F (205°C). Roll out the dough, on parchment paper, into a rectangle, then cut it into 8 strips. Whisk the baking soda and 1 cup of hot water until well dissolved in a bowl. Submerge each strip, shake off any excess, and stretch another 1 to 2 inches. Scatter with caraway seeds and let rise for 10 minutes in the frying basket. Grease with cooking spray and Air Fry for 8 minutes until golden brown, turning once. Serve.

Flatbread Dippers

Servings: 12
Cooking Time: 8 Minutes
Ingredients:
- 1 cup shredded mozzarella cheese
- 1 ounce cream cheese, broken into small pieces
- ½ cup blanched finely ground almond flour

Directions:
1. Place mozzarella into a large microwave-safe bowl. Add cream cheese pieces. Microwave on high 60 seconds, then stir to combine. Add flour and stir until a soft ball of dough forms.
2. Cut dough ball into two equal pieces. Cut a piece of parchment to fit into air fryer basket. Press each dough piece into a 5" round on ungreased parchment.
3. Place parchment with dough into air fryer basket. Adjust the temperature to 350°F (175°C) and set the timer for 8 minutes. Carefully flip the flatbread over halfway through cooking. Flatbread will be golden brown when done.
4. Let flatbread cool 5 minutes, then slice each round into six triangles. Serve warm.

Ninja Air Fryer Cookbook

Chapter 4: Appetizers And Snacks

Honey Tater Tots With Bacon

Servings: 4
Cooking Time: 25 Minutes
Ingredients:
- 24 frozen tater tots
- 6 bacon slices
- 1 tbsp honey
- 1 cup grated cheddar

Directions:
1. Preheat air fryer to 400°F (205°C). Air Fry the tater tots for 10 minutes, shaking the basket once halfway through cooking. Cut the bacon into pieces. When the tater tots are done, remove them from the fryer to a baking pan. Top them with bacon and drizzle with honey. Air Fry for 5 minutes to crisp up the bacon. Top the tater tots with cheese and cook for 2 minutes to melt the cheese. Serve.

Pickled Chips

Servings: 4
Cooking Time: 10 Minutes
Ingredients:
- 1 cup pickles, sliced
- 2 eggs, beaten
- ½ cup coconut flakes
- 1 teaspoon dried cilantro
- ¼ cup Provolone cheese, grated

Directions:
1. Mix up coconut flakes, dried cilantro, and Provolone cheese. Then dip the sliced pickles in the egg and coat in coconut flakes mixture. Preheat the air fryer to 400°F (205°C). Arrange the pickles in the air fryer in one layer and cook them for 5 minutes. Then flip the pickles on another side and cook for another 5 minutes.

Garlic Breadsticks

Servings: 12
Cooking Time: 7 Minutes
Ingredients:
- 1½ tablespoons Olive oil
- 1½ teaspoons Minced garlic
- ¼ teaspoon Table salt
- ¼ teaspoon Ground black pepper
- 6 ounces Purchased pizza dough (vegan dough, if that's a concern)

Directions:
1. Preheat the air fryer to 400°F (205°C). Mix the oil, garlic, salt, and pepper in a small bowl.
2. Divide the pizza dough into 4 balls for a small air fryer, 6 for a medium machine, or 8 for a large, each ball about the size of a walnut in its shell. Roll each ball into a 5-inch-long stick under your clean palms on a clean, dry work surface. Brush the sticks with the oil mixture.
3. When the machine is at temperature, place the prepared dough sticks in the basket, leaving a 1-inch space between them. Air-fry undisturbed for 7 minutes, or until puffed, golden, and set to the touch.
4. Use kitchen tongs to gently transfer the breadsticks to a wire rack and repeat step 3 with the remaining dough sticks.

Basil Pork Bites

Servings: 6
Cooking Time: 25 Minutes
Ingredients:
- 2 pounds pork belly, cut into strips
- 2 tablespoons olive oil
- 2 teaspoons fennel seeds
- A pinch of salt and black pepper
- A pinch of basil, dried

Directions:
1. In a bowl, mix all the ingredients, toss and put the pork strips in your air fryer's basket and cook at 425°F (220°C) for 25 minutes. Divide into bowls and serve as a snack.

Home-style Taro Chips

Servings: 2
Cooking Time: 20 Minutes
Ingredients:
- 1 tbsp olive oil
- 1 cup thinly sliced taro
- Salt to taste
- ½ cup hummus

Directions:
1. Preheat air fryer to 325°F (220°C). Put the sliced taro in the greased frying basket, spread the pieces out, and drizzle with olive oil. Air Fry for 10-12 minutes, shaking the basket twice. Sprinkle with salt and serve with hummus.

Rumaki

Servings: 24
Cooking Time: 12 Minutes
Ingredients:
- 10 ounces raw chicken livers
- 1 can sliced water chestnuts, drained
- ¼ cup low-sodium teriyaki sauce
- 12 slices turkey bacon
- toothpicks

Directions:
1. Cut livers into 1½-inch pieces, trimming out tough veins as you slice.
2. Place livers, water chestnuts, and teriyaki sauce in small container with lid. If needed, add another tablespoon of teriyaki sauce to make sure livers are covered. Refrigerate for 1 hour.
3. When ready to cook, cut bacon slices in half crosswise.
4. Wrap 1 piece of liver and 1 slice of water chestnut in each bacon strip. Secure with toothpick.
5. When you have wrapped half of the livers, place them in the air fryer basket in a single layer.
6. Cook at 390°F (200°C) for 12 minutes, until liver is done and bacon is crispy.
7. While first batch cooks, wrap the remaining livers. Repeat step 6 to cook your second batch.

Roasted Peppers

Servings: 4
Cooking Time: 40 Minutes
Ingredients:
- 12 medium bell peppers
- 1 sweet onion, small
- 1 tbsp. Maggi sauce
- 1 tbsp. extra virgin olive oil

Directions:
1. Warm up the olive oil and Maggi sauce in Air Fryer at 320°F (160°C).
2. Peel the onion, slice it into 1-inch pieces, and add it to the Air Fryer.
3. Wash and de-stem the peppers. Slice them into 1-inch pieces and remove all the seeds, with water if necessary.
4. Place the peppers in the Air Fryer.
5. Cook for about 25 minutes, or longer if desired. Serve hot.

Grilled Cheese Sandwich Deluxe

Servings: 4
Cooking Time: 6 Minutes
Ingredients:
- 8 ounces Brie
- 8 slices oat nut bread
- 1 large ripe pear, cored and cut into ½-inch-thick slices
- 2 tablespoons butter, melted

Directions:
1. Spread a quarter of the Brie on each of four slices of bread.
2. Top Brie with thick slices of pear, then the remaining 4 slices of bread.
3. Lightly brush both sides of each sandwich with melted butter.
4. Cooking 2 at a time, place sandwiches in air fryer basket and cook at 360°F (180°C) for 6 minutes or until cheese melts and outside looks golden brown.

Cinnamon Apple Crisps

Servings: 1
Cooking Time: 22 Minutes
Ingredients:
- 1 large apple
- ½ teaspoon ground cinnamon
- 2 teaspoons avocado oil or coconut oil

Directions:
1. Preheat the air fryer to 300°F (150°C).
2. Using a mandolin or knife, slice the apples to ¼-inch thickness. Pat the apples dry with a paper towel or kitchen cloth. Sprinkle the apple slices with ground cinnamon. Spray or drizzle the oil over the top of the apple slices and toss to coat.
3. Place the apple slices in the air fryer basket. To allow for even cooking, don't overlap the slices; cook in batches if necessary.
4. Cook for 20 minutes, shaking the basket every 5 minutes. After 20 minutes, increase the air fryer temperature to 330°F (165°C) and cook another 2 minutes, shaking the basket every 30 seconds. Remove the apples from the basket before they get too dark.
5. Spread the chips out onto paper towels to cool completely, at least 5 minutes. Repeat with the remaining apple slices until they're all cooked.

Cheddar Cheese Lumpia Rolls

Servings: 5
Cooking Time: 20 Minutes
Ingredients:
- 5 ounces mature cheddar cheese, cut into 15 sticks
- 15 pieces spring roll lumpia wrappers
- 2 tablespoons sesame oil

Directions:
1. Wrap the cheese sticks in the lumpia wrappers. Transfer to the Air Fryer basket. Brush with sesame oil.
2. Bake in the preheated Air Fryer at 395°F (200°C) for 10 minutes or until the lumpia wrappers turn golden brown. Work in batches.
3. Shake the Air Fryer basket occasionally to ensure even cooking. Bon appétit!

Fried Goat Cheese

Servings: 3
Cooking Time: 4 Minutes
Ingredients:
- 7 ounces 1- to 1½-inch-diameter goat cheese log
- 2 Large egg(s)
- 1¾ cups Plain dried bread crumbs (gluten-free, if a concern)
- Vegetable oil spray

Directions:
1. Slice the goat cheese log into ½-inch-thick rounds. Set these flat on a small cutting board, a small baking sheet, or a large plate. Freeze uncovered for 30 minutes.
2. Preheat the air fryer to 400°F (205°C).
3. Set up and fill two shallow soup plates or small pie plates on your counter: one in which you whisk the egg(s) until uniform and the other for the bread crumbs.
4. Take the goat cheese rounds out of the freezer. With clean, dry hands, dip one round in the egg(s) to coat it on all sides. Let the excess egg slip back into the rest, then dredge the round in the bread crumbs, turning it to coat all sides, even the edges. Repeat this process—egg, then bread crumbs—for a second coating. Coat both sides of the round and its edges with vegetable oil spray, then set it aside. Continue double-dipping, double-dredging, and spraying the remaining rounds.
5. Place the rounds in one layer in the basket. Air-fry undisturbed for 4 minutes, or until lightly browned and crunchy. Do not overcook. Some of the goat cheese may break through the crust. A few little breaks are fine but stop the cooking before the coating reaches structural failure.
6. Remove the basket from the machine and set aside for 3 minutes. Use a nonstick-safe spatula, and maybe a flatware fork for balance, to transfer the rounds to a wire rack. Cool for 5 minutes more before serving.

Bacon & Blue Cheese Tartlets

Servings: 6
Cooking Time: 30 Minutes
Ingredients:
- 6 bacon slices
- 16 phyllo tartlet shells
- ½ cup diced blue cheese
- 3 tbsp apple jelly

Directions:
1. Preheat the air fryer to 400°F (205°C). Put the bacon in a single layer in the frying basket and Air Fry for 14 minutes, turning once halfway through. Remove and drain on paper towels, then crumble when cool. Wipe the fryer clean. Fill the tartlet shells with bacon and the blue cheese cubes and add a dab of apple jelly on top of the filling. Lower the temperature to 350°F (175°C), then put the shells in the frying basket. Air Fry until the cheese melts and the shells brown, about 5-6 minutes. Remove and serve.

Bacon-wrapped Jalapeño Poppers

Servings: 4
Cooking Time: 12 Minutes
Ingredients:
- 3 ounces full-fat cream cheese
- ½ cup shredded sharp Cheddar cheese
- ¼ teaspoon garlic powder
- 6 jalapeño peppers, trimmed and halved lengthwise, seeded and membranes removed
- 12 slices bacon

Directions:
1. Preheat the air fryer to 400°F (205°C).
2. In a large microwave-safe bowl, place cream cheese, Cheddar, and garlic powder. Microwave 20 seconds until softened and stir. Spoon cheese mixture into hollow jalapeño halves.
3. Wrap a bacon slice around each jalapeño half, completely covering pepper.
4. Place in the air fryer basket and cook 12 minutes, turning halfway through cooking time. Serve warm.

Veggie Chips

Servings: X
Cooking Time: X
Ingredients:
- sweet potato
- large parsnip
- large carrot
- turnip
- large beet
- vegetable or canola oil, in a spray bottle
- salt

Directions:
1. You can do a medley of vegetable chips, or just select from the vegetables listed. Whatever you choose to do, scrub the vegetables well and then slice them paper-thin using a mandolin.
2. Preheat the air fryer to 400°F (205°C).
3. Air-fry the chips in batches, one type of vegetable at a time. Spray the chips lightly with oil and transfer them to the air fryer basket. The key is to NOT over-load the basket. You can overlap the chips a little, but don't pile them on top of each other. Doing so will make it much harder to get evenly browned and crispy chips. Air-fry at 400°F (205°C) for the time indicated below, shaking the basket several times during the cooking process for even cooking.
4. Sweet Potato – 8 to 9 minutes
5. Parsnips – 5 minutes
6. Carrot – 7 minutes
7. Turnips – 8 minutes
8. Beets – 9 minutes
9. Season the chips with salt during the last couple of minutes of air-frying. Check the chips as they cook until they are done to your liking. Some will start to brown sooner than others.
10. You can enjoy the chips warm out of the air fryer or cool them to room temperature for crispier chips.

Apple Rollups

Servings: 8
Cooking Time: 5 Minutes
Ingredients:
- 8 slices whole wheat sandwich bread
- 4 ounces Colby Jack cheese, grated
- ½ small apple, chopped
- 2 tablespoons butter, melted

Directions:
1. Remove crusts from bread and flatten the slices with rolling pin. Don't be gentle. Press hard so that bread will be very thin.
2. Top bread slices with cheese and chopped apple, dividing the ingredients evenly.
3. Roll up each slice tightly and secure each with one or two toothpicks.
4. Brush outside of rolls with melted butter.
5. Place in air fryer basket and cook at 390°F (200°C) for 5minutes, until outside is crisp and nicely browned.

Okra Chips

Servings: 4
Cooking Time: 16 Minutes
Ingredients:
- 1¼ pounds Thin fresh okra pods, cut into 1-inch pieces
- 1½ tablespoons Vegetable or canola oil
- ¾ teaspoon Coarse sea salt or kosher salt

Directions:
1. Preheat the air fryer to 400°F (205°C).
2. Toss the okra, oil, and salt in a large bowl until the pieces are well and evenly coated.
3. When the machine is at temperature, pour the contents of the bowl into the basket. Air-fry, tossing several times, for 16 minutes, or until crisp and quite brown.
4. Pour the contents of the basket onto a wire rack. Cool for a couple of minutes before serving.

Cauliflower Buns

Servings: 8
Cooking Time: 12 Minutes
Ingredients:
- 1 steamer bag cauliflower, cooked according to package instructions
- ½ cup shredded mozzarella cheese
- ¼ cup shredded mild Cheddar cheese
- ¼ cup blanched finely ground almond flour
- 1 large egg
- ½ teaspoon salt

Directions:
1. Let cooked cauliflower cool about 10 minutes. Use a kitchen towel to wring out excess moisture, then place cauliflower in a food processor.
2. Add mozzarella, Cheddar, flour, egg, and salt to the food processor and pulse twenty times until mixture is combined. It will resemble a soft, wet dough.
3. Divide mixture into eight piles. Wet your hands with water to prevent sticking, then press each pile into a flat bun shape, about ½" thick.
4. Cut a sheet of parchment to fit air fryer basket. Working in batches if needed, place the formed dough onto ungreased parchment in air fryer basket. Adjust the temperature to 350°F (175°C) and set the timer for 12 minutes, turning buns halfway through cooking.
5. Let buns cool 10 minutes before serving. Serve warm.

Lemon Tofu Cubes

Servings: 2
Cooking Time: 7 Minutes
Ingredients:
- ½ teaspoon ground coriander
- 1 tablespoon avocado oil
- 1 teaspoon lemon juice
- ½ teaspoon chili flakes
- 6 oz tofu

Directions:
1. In the shallow bowl mix up ground coriander, avocado oil, lemon juice, and chili flakes. Chop the tofu into cubes and sprinkle with coriander mixture. Shake the tofu. After this, preheat the air fryer to 400°F (205°C) and put the tofu cubes in it. Cook the tofu for 4 minutes. Then flip the tofu on another side and cook for 3 minutes more.

Thyme Sweet Potato Chips

Servings: 2
Cooking Time: 20 Minutes
Ingredients:
- 1 tbsp olive oil
- 1 sweet potato, sliced
- ¼ tsp dried thyme
- Salt to taste

Directions:
1. Preheat air fryer to 390°F (200°C). Spread the sweet potato slices in the greased basket and brush with olive oil. Air Fry for 6 minutes. Remove the basket, shake, and sprinkle with thyme and salt. Cook for 6 more minutes or until lightly browned. Serve warm and enjoy!

Root Vegetable Crisps

Servings: 4
Cooking Time: 8 Minutes
Ingredients:
- 1 small taro root, peeled and washed
- 1 small yucca root, peeled and washed
- 1 small purple sweet potato, washed
- 2 cups filtered water
- 2 teaspoons extra-virgin olive oil
- ½ teaspoon salt

Directions:
1. Using a mandolin, slice the taro root, yucca root, and purple sweet potato into ⅛-inch slices.
2. Add the water to a large bowl. Add the sliced vegetables and soak for at least 30 minutes.
3. Preheat the air fryer to 370°F (185°C).
4. Drain the water and pat the vegetables dry with a paper towel or kitchen cloth. Toss the vegetables with the olive oil and sprinkle with salt. Liberally spray the air fryer basket with olive oil mist.
5. Place the vegetables into the air fryer basket, making sure not to overlap the pieces.
6. Cook for 8 minutes, shaking the basket every 2 minutes, until the outer edges start to turn up and the vegetables start to brown. Remove from the basket and serve warm. Repeat with the remaining vegetable slices until all are cooked.

Sweet Apple Fries

Servings: 3
Cooking Time: 8 Minutes
Ingredients:
- 2 Medium-size sweet apple(s), such as Gala or Fuji
- 1 Large egg white(s)
- 2 tablespoons Water
- 1½ cups Finely ground gingersnap crumbs (gluten-free, if a concern)
- Vegetable oil spray

Directions:
1. Preheat the air fryer to 375°F (190°C).
2. Peel and core an apple, then cut it into 12 slices. Repeat with more apples as necessary.
3. Whisk the egg white(s) and water in a medium bowl until foamy. Add the apple slices and toss well to coat.
4. Spread the gingersnap crumbs across a dinner plate. Using clean hands, pick up an apple slice, let any excess egg white mixture slip back into the rest, and dredge the slice in the crumbs, coating it lightly but evenly on all sides. Set it aside and continue coating the remaining apple slices.
5. Lightly coat the slices on all sides with vegetable oil spray, then set them curved side down in the basket in one layer. Air-fry undisturbed for 6 minutes, or until browned and crisp. You may need to air-fry the slices for 2 minutes longer if the temperature is at 360°F (180°C).
6. Use kitchen tongs to transfer the slices to a wire rack. Cool for 2 to 3 minutes before serving.

Za'atar Garbanzo Beans

Servings: 6
Cooking Time: 12 Minutes
Ingredients:
- One 14.5-ounce can garbanzo beans, drained and rinsed
- 1 tablespoon extra-virgin olive oil
- 6 teaspoons za'atar seasoning mix
- 2 tablespoons chopped parsley
- Salt and pepper, to taste

Directions:
1. Preheat the air fryer to 390°F (200°C).
2. In a medium bowl, toss the garbanzo beans with olive oil and za'atar seasoning.
3. Pour the beans into the air fryer basket and cook for 12 minutes, or until toasted as you like. Stir every 3 minutes while roasting.
4. Remove the beans from the air fryer basket into a serving bowl, top with fresh chopped parsley, and season with salt and pepper.

Mexican Muffins

Servings: 4
Cooking Time: 15 Minutes
Ingredients:
- 1 cup ground beef
- 1 teaspoon taco seasonings
- 2 oz Mexican blend cheese, shredded
- 1 teaspoon keto tomato sauce
- Cooking spray

Directions:
1. Preheat the air fryer to 375°F (190°C). Meanwhile, in the mixing bowl mix up ground beef and taco seasonings. Spray the muffin molds with cooking spray. Then transfer the ground beef mixture in the muffin molds and top them with cheese and tomato sauce. Transfer the muffin molds in the preheated air fryer and cook them for 15 minutes.

Cheesy Tortellini Bites

Servings: 8
Cooking Time: 10 Minutes
Ingredients:
- 1 large egg
- ½ teaspoon black pepper
- ½ teaspoon garlic powder
- 1 teaspoon Italian seasoning
- 12 ounces frozen cheese tortellini
- ½ cup panko breadcrumbs

Directions:
1. Preheat the air fryer to 380°F (195°C).
2. Spray the air fryer basket with an olive-oil-based spray.
3. In a medium bowl, whisk the egg with the pepper, garlic powder, and Italian seasoning.
4. Dip the tortellini in the egg batter and then coat with the breadcrumbs. Place each tortellini in the basket, trying not to overlap them. You may need to cook in batches to ensure the even crisp all around.
5. Bake for 5 minutes, shake the basket, and bake another 5 minutes.
6. Remove and let cool 5 minutes. Serve with marinara sauce, ranch, or your favorite dressing.

Roasted Chickpeas

Servings: 1
Cooking Time: 15 Minutes
Ingredients:
- 1 15-ounce can chickpeas, drained
- 2 teaspoons curry powder
- ¼ teaspoon salt
- 1 tablespoon olive oil

Directions:
1. Drain chickpeas thoroughly and spread in a single layer on paper towels. Cover with another paper towel and press gently to remove extra moisture. Don't press too hard or you'll crush the chickpeas.
2. Mix curry powder and salt together.
3. Place chickpeas in a medium bowl and sprinkle with seasonings. Stir well to coat.
4. Add olive oil and stir again to distribute oil.
5. Cook at 390°F (200°C) for 15 minutes, stopping to shake basket about halfway through cooking time.
6. Cool completely and store in airtight container.

Eggs In Avocado Halves

Servings: 3
Cooking Time: 23 Minutes
Ingredients:
- 3 Hass avocados, halved and pitted but not peeled
- 6 Medium eggs
- Vegetable oil spray
- 3 tablespoons Heavy or light cream (not fat-free cream)
- To taste Table salt
- To taste Ground black pepper

Directions:
1. Preheat the air fryer to 350°F (175°C).
2. Slice a small amount off the (skin) side of each avocado half so it can sit stable, without rocking. Lightly coat the skin of the avocado half with vegetable oil spray.
3. Arrange the avocado halves open side up on a cutting board, then crack an egg into the indentation in each where the pit had been. If any white overflows the avocado half, wipe that bit of white off the cut edge of the avocado before proceeding.
4. Remove the basket (or its attachment) from the machine and set the filled avocado halves in it in one layer. Return it to the machine without pushing it in. Drizzle each avocado half with about 1½ teaspoons cream, a little salt, and a little ground black pepper.
5. Air-fry undisturbed for 10 minutes for a soft-set yolk, or air-fry for 13 minutes for more-set eggs.
6. Use a nonstick-safe spatula and a flatware fork for balance to transfer the avocado halves to serving plates. Cool a minute or two before serving.

Bacon-wrapped Cabbage Bites

Servings: 6
Cooking Time: 12 Minutes
Ingredients:
- 3 tablespoons sriracha hot chili sauce, divided
- 1 medium head cabbage, cored and cut into 12 bite-sized pieces
- 2 tablespoons coconut oil, melted
- ½ teaspoon salt
- 12 slices sugar-free bacon
- ½ cup mayonnaise
- ¼ teaspoon garlic powder

Directions:
1. Evenly brush 2 tablespoons sriracha onto cabbage pieces. Drizzle evenly with coconut oil, then sprinkle with salt.
2. Wrap each cabbage piece with bacon and secure with a toothpick. Place into ungreased air fryer basket. Adjust the temperature to 375°F (190°C) and set the timer for 12 minutes, turning cabbage halfway through cooking. Bacon will be cooked and crispy when done.
3. In a small bowl, whisk together mayonnaise, garlic powder, and remaining sriracha. Use as a dipping sauce for cabbage bites.

Amazing Blooming Onion

Servings: 4
Cooking Time: 40 Minutes
Ingredients:
- 4 medium/small onions
- 1 tbsp. olive oil
- 4 dollops of butter

Directions:
1. Peel the onion. Cut off the top and bottom.
2. To make it bloom, cut as deeply as possible without slicing through it completely. 4 cuts should do it.
3. Place the onions in a bowl of salted water and allow to absorb for 4 hours to help eliminate the sharp taste and induce the blooming process.
4. Pre-heat your Air Fryer to 355°F (180°C).
5. Transfer the onions to the Air Fryer. Pour over a light drizzle of olive oil and place a dollop of butter on top of each onion.
6. Cook or roast for 30 minutes. Remove the outer layer before serving if it is too brown.

Bacon-wrapped Goat Cheese Poppers

Servings: 10
Cooking Time: 10 Minutes
Ingredients:
- 10 large jalapeño peppers
- 8 ounces goat cheese
- 10 slices bacon

Directions:
1. Preheat the air fryer to 380°F (175°C).
2. Slice the jalapeños in half. Carefully remove the veins and seeds of the jalapeños with a spoon.
3. Fill each jalapeño half with 2 teaspoons goat cheese.
4. Cut the bacon in half lengthwise to make long strips. Wrap the jalapeños with bacon, trying to cover the entire length of the jalapeño.
5. Place the bacon-wrapped jalapeños into the air fryer basket. Cook the stuffed jalapeños for 10 minutes or until bacon is crispy.

Fried Ranch Pickles

Servings: 4
Cooking Time: 10 Minutes
Ingredients:
- 4 dill pickle spears, halved lengthwise
- ¼ cup ranch dressing
- ½ cup blanched finely ground almond flour
- ½ cup grated Parmesan cheese
- 2 tablespoons dry ranch seasoning

Directions:
1. Wrap spears in a kitchen towel 30 minutes to soak up excess pickle juice.
2. Pour ranch dressing into a medium bowl and add pickle spears. In a separate medium bowl, mix flour, Parmesan, and ranch seasoning.
3. Remove each spear from ranch dressing and shake off excess. Press gently into dry mixture to coat all sides. Place spears into ungreased air fryer basket. Adjust the temperature to 400°F (205°C) and set the timer for 10 minutes, turning spears three times during cooking. Serve warm.

Ninja Air Fryer Cookbook

Chapter 5: Bread And Breakfast

Black's Bangin' Casserole

Servings: 4
Cooking Time: 40 Minutes
Ingredients:
- 5 eggs
- 3 tbsp chunky tomato sauce
- 2 tbsp heavy cream
- 2 tbsp grated parmesan cheese

Directions:
1. Preheat your fryer to 350°F (175°C)
2. Combine the eggs and cream in a bowl.
3. Mix in the tomato sauce and add the cheese.
4. Spread into a glass baking dish and bake for 25-35 minutes.
5. Top with extra cheese.
6. Enjoy!

Crispy Bacon

Servings: 6
Cooking Time: 20 Minutes
Ingredients:
- 12 ounces bacon

Directions:
1. Preheat the air fryer to 350°F (175°C) for 3 minutes.
2. Lay out the bacon in a single layer, slightly overlapping the strips of bacon.
3. Air fry for 10 minutes or until desired crispness.
4. Repeat until all the bacon has been cooked.

Tuna And Arugula Salad

Servings: 4
Cooking Time: 15 Minutes
Ingredients:
- ½ pound smoked tuna, flaked
- 1 cup arugula
- 2 spring onions, chopped
- 1 tablespoon olive oil
- A pinch of salt and black pepper

Directions:
1. In a bowl, all the ingredients except the oil and the arugula and whisk. Preheat the Air Fryer over 360°F (180°C), add the oil and grease it. Pour the tuna mix, stir well, and cook for 15 minutes. In a salad bowl, combine the arugula with the tuna mix, toss and serve for breakfast.

Cinnamon Rolls

Servings: 12
Cooking Time: 20 Minutes
Ingredients:
- 2½ cups shredded mozzarella cheese
- 2 ounces cream cheese, softened
- 1 cup blanched finely ground almond flour
- ½ teaspoon vanilla extract
- ½ cup confectioners' erythritol
- 1 tablespoon ground cinnamon

Directions:
1. In a large microwave-safe bowl, combine mozzarella cheese, cream cheese, and flour. Microwave the mixture on high 90 seconds until cheese is melted.
2. Add vanilla extract and erythritol, and mix 2 minutes until a dough forms.
3. Once the dough is cool enough to work with your hands, about 2 minutes, spread it out into a 12" × 4" rectangle on ungreased parchment paper. Evenly sprinkle dough with cinnamon.
4. Starting at the long side of the dough, roll lengthwise to form a log. Slice the log into twelve even pieces.
5. Divide rolls between two ungreased 6" round nonstick baking dishes. Place one dish into air fryer basket. Adjust the temperature to 375°F (190°C) and set the timer for 10 minutes.
6. Cinnamon rolls will be done when golden around the edges and mostly firm. Repeat with second dish. Allow rolls to cool in dishes 10 minutes before serving.

Very Berry Breakfast Puffs

Servings: 3
Cooking Time: 20 Minutes
Ingredients:
- 2 tbsp mashed strawberries
- 2 tbsp mashed raspberries
- ¼ tsp vanilla extract
- 2 cups cream cheese
- 1 tbsp honey

Directions:
1. Preheat the air fryer to 375°F (190C). Divide the cream cheese between the dough sheets and spread it evenly. In a small bowl, combine the berries, honey and vanilla.
2. Divide the mixture between the pastry sheets. Pinch the ends of the sheets, to form puff. Place the puffs on a lined baking dish. Place the dish in the air fryer and cook for 15 minutes.

Egg In A Hole

Servings: 4
Cooking Time: 10 Minutes
Ingredients:
- 4 slices white sandwich bread
- 4 large eggs
- ½ teaspoon salt
- ¼ teaspoon ground black pepper

Directions:
1. Preheat the air fryer to 350°F (175°C). Spray a 6" round cake pan with cooking spray.
2. Place as many pieces of bread as will fit in one layer in prepared pan, working in batches as necessary.
3. Using a small cup or cookie cutter, cut a circle out of the center of each bread slice. Crack an egg directly into each cutout and sprinkle eggs with salt and pepper.
4. Cook 5 minutes, then carefully turn and cook an additional 5 minutes or less, depending on your preference. Serve warm.

Chocolate-hazelnut Bear Claws

Servings: 4
Cooking Time: 10 Minutes
Ingredients:
- 1 sheet frozen puff pastry dough, thawed
- 1 large egg, beaten
- ½ cup chocolate-hazelnut spread
- 1 tablespoon confectioners' sugar
- 1 tablespoon sliced almonds

Directions:
1. Preheat the air fryer to 320°F (160°C).
2. Unfold puff pastry and cut into four equal squares.
3. Brush egg evenly over puff pastry.
4. To make each bear claw, spread 2 tablespoons chocolate-hazelnut spread over a pastry square. Fold square horizontally to form a triangle and cut four evenly spaced slits about halfway through the top of folded square. Repeat with remaining spread and pastry squares.
5. Sprinkle confectioners' sugar and almonds over bear claws and place directly in the air fryer basket. Cook 10 minutes until puffy and golden brown. Serve warm.

Chocolate Chip Scones

Servings: 8
Cooking Time: 15 Minutes
Ingredients:
- ½ cup cold salted butter, divided
- 2 cups all-purpose flour
- ½ cup brown sugar
- ½ teaspoon baking powder
- 1 large egg
- ¾ cup buttermilk
- ½ cup semisweet chocolate chips

Directions:
1. Preheat the air fryer to 320°F (160°C). Cut parchment paper to fit the air fryer basket.
2. Chill 6 tablespoons butter in the freezer 10 minutes. In a small microwave-safe bowl, microwave remaining 2 tablespoons butter 30 seconds until melted, and set aside.
3. In a large bowl, mix flour, brown sugar, and baking powder.
4. Remove butter from freezer and grate into bowl. Use a wooden spoon to evenly distribute.
5. Add egg and buttermilk and stir gently until a soft, sticky dough forms. Gently fold in chocolate chips.
6. Turn dough out onto a lightly floured surface. Fold a couple of times and gently form into a 6" round. Cut into eight triangles.
7. Place scones on parchment in the air fryer basket, leaving at least 2" space between each, working in batches as necessary.
8. Brush each scone with melted butter. Cook 15 minutes until scones are dark golden brown and crispy on the edges, and a toothpick inserted into the center comes out clean. Serve warm.

Spinach-bacon Rollups

Servings: 4
Cooking Time: 9 Minutes
Ingredients:
- 4 flour tortillas
- 4 slices Swiss cheese
- 1 cup baby spinach leaves
- 4 slices turkey bacon

Directions:
1. Preheat air fryer to 390°F (200°C).
2. On each tortilla, place one slice of cheese and ¼ cup of spinach.
3. Roll up tortillas and wrap each with a strip of bacon. Secure each end with a toothpick.
4. Place rollups in air fryer basket, leaving a little space in between them.
5. Cook for 4 minutes. Turn and rearrange rollups and cook for 5 minutes longer, until bacon is crisp.

Blueberry Scones

Servings: 8
Cooking Time: 15 Minutes
Ingredients:
- ½ cup cold salted butter, divided
- 2 cups all-purpose flour
- ½ cup granulated sugar
- 1 teaspoon baking powder
- 1 large egg
- ½ cup whole milk
- ½ cup fresh blueberries

Directions:
1. Chill 6 tablespoons butter in the freezer 10 minutes. In a small microwave-safe bowl, microwave remaining 2 tablespoons butter 30 seconds until melted.
2. Preheat the air fryer to 320°F (160°C). Cut parchment paper to fit the air fryer basket.
3. In a large bowl, mix flour, sugar, and baking powder.
4. Add egg and milk and stir until a sticky dough forms.
5. Remove butter from freezer and grate into bowl. Fold grated butter into dough until just combined.
6. Fold in blueberries. Turn dough onto a lightly floured surface. Sprinkle dough with flour and fold a couple of times, then gently form into a 6" round. Cut into eight triangles.
7. Place scones on parchment in the air fryer basket, leaving at least 2" of space between each, working in batches as necessary.
8. Brush each scone with melted butter and cook 15 minutes until scones are dark golden brown and crispy on the edges, and a toothpick inserted into the center comes out clean. Serve warm.

Onion Marinated Skirt Steak

Servings: 3
Cooking Time: 45 Minutes
Ingredients:
- 1 large red onion, grated or pureed
- 2 tablespoons brown sugar
- 1 tablespoon vinegar
- 1 ½ pounds skirt steak

Ninja Air Fryer Cookbook

- Salt and pepper to taste

Directions:
1. Place all ingredients in a Ziploc bag and allow to marinate in the fridge for at least 2 hours.
2. Preheat the air fryer at 390°F (200°C).
3. Place the grill pan accessory in the air fryer.
4. Grill for 15 minutes per batch.
5. Flip every 8 minutes for even grilling.

Mediterranean Egg Sandwich

Servings: 1
Cooking Time: 8 Minutes
Ingredients:
- 1 large egg
- 5 baby spinach leaves, chopped
- 1 tablespoon roasted bell pepper, chopped
- 1 English muffin
- 1 thin slice prosciutto or Canadian bacon

Directions:
1. Spray a ramekin with cooking spray or brush the inside with extra-virgin olive oil.
2. In a small bowl, whisk together the egg, baby spinach, and bell pepper.
3. Split the English muffin in half and spray the inside lightly with cooking spray or brush with extra-virgin olive oil.
4. Preheat the air fryer to 350°F (175°C) for 2 minutes. Place the egg ramekin and open English muffin into the air fryer basket, and cook at 350°F (175°C) for 5 minutes. Open the air fryer drawer and add the prosciutto or bacon; cook for an additional 1 minute.
5. To assemble the sandwich, place the egg on one half of the English muffin, top with prosciutto or bacon, and place the remaining piece of English muffin on top.

Meaty Omelet

Servings: 4
Cooking Time: 20 Minutes
Ingredients:
- 6 eggs
- ½ cup grated Swiss cheese
- 3 breakfast sausages, sliced
- 8 bacon strips, sliced
- Salt and pepper to taste

Directions:
1. Preheat air fryer to 360°F (180°C). In a bowl, beat the eggs and stir in Swiss cheese, sausages and bacon. Transfer the mixture to a baking dish and set in the fryer. Bake for 15 minutes or until golden and crisp. Season and serve.

Bacon Eggs

Servings: 2
Cooking Time: 5 Minutes
Ingredients:
- 2 eggs, hard-boiled, peeled
- 4 bacon slices
- ½ teaspoon avocado oil
- 1 teaspoon mustard

Directions:
1. Preheat the air fryer to 400°F (205°C). Then sprinkle the air fryer basket with avocado oil and place the bacon slices inside. Flatten them in one layer and cook for 2 minutes from each side. After this, cool the bacon to the room temperature. Wrap every egg into 2 bacon slices. Secure the eggs with toothpicks and place them in the air fryer. Cook the wrapped eggs for 1 minute at 400°F (205°C).

Cheese Pie

Servings: 4
Cooking Time: 16 Minutes
Ingredients:
- 8 eggs
- 1 1/2 cups heavy whipping cream
- 1 lb cheddar cheese, grated
- Pepper
- Salt

Directions:
1. Preheat the air fryer to 325°F (160°C).
2. In a bowl, whisk together cheese, eggs, whipping cream, pepper, and salt.
3. Spray air fryer baking dish with cooking spray.
4. Pour egg mixture into the prepared dish and place in the air fryer basket.
5. Cook for 16 minutes or until the egg is set.
6. Serve and enjoy.

Oregano And Coconut Scramble

Servings: 4
Cooking Time: 20 Minutes
Ingredients:
- 8 eggs, whisked
- 2 tablespoons oregano, chopped
- Salt and black pepper to the taste
- 2 tablespoons parmesan, grated
- ¼ cup coconut cream

Directions:
1. In a bowl, mix the eggs with all the ingredients and whisk. Pour this into a pan that fits your air fryer, introduce it in the preheated fryer and cook at 350°F (175°C) for 20 minutes, stirring often. Divide the scramble between plates and serve for breakfast.

Bacon And Cheese Quiche

Servings: 2
Cooking Time: 12 Minutes
Ingredients:
- 3 large eggs
- 2 tablespoons heavy whipping cream
- ¼ teaspoon salt
- 4 slices cooked sugar-free bacon, crumbled
- ½ cup shredded mild Cheddar cheese

Directions:
1. In a large bowl, whisk eggs, cream, and salt together until combined. Mix in bacon and Cheddar.
2. Pour mixture evenly into two ungreased 4" ramekins. Place into air fryer basket. Adjust the temperature to 320°F (160°C) and set the timer for 12 minutes. Quiche will be fluffy and set in the middle when done.
3. Let quiche cool in ramekins 5 minutes. Serve warm.

Bagels

Servings: 4
Cooking Time: 10 Minutes
Ingredients:
- 1 cup self-rising flour
- 1 cup plain full-fat Greek yogurt
- 2 tablespoons granulated sugar
- 1 large egg, whisked

Directions:
1. Preheat the air fryer to 320°F (160°C).
2. In a large bowl, mix flour, yogurt, and sugar together until a ball of dough forms.
3. Turn dough out onto a lightly floured surface. Knead dough for 3 minutes, then form into a smooth ball. Cut dough into four sections. Roll each piece into an 8" rope, then shape into a circular bagel shape. Brush top and bottom of each bagel with egg.
4. Place in the air fryer basket and cook 10 minutes, turning halfway through cooking time to ensure even browning. Let cool 5 minutes before serving.

Blueberry Muffins

Servings: 12
Cooking Time: 15 Minutes
Ingredients:
- 1 cup all-purpose flour
- ½ cup granulated sugar
- 1 teaspoon baking powder
- ¼ cup salted butter, melted
- 1 large egg
- ½ cup whole milk
- 1 cup fresh blueberries

Directions:
1. Preheat the air fryer to 300°F (150°C).
2. In a large bowl, whisk together flour, sugar, and baking powder.
3. Add butter, egg, and milk to dry mixture. Stir until well combined.
4. Gently fold in blueberries. Divide batter evenly among twelve silicone or aluminum muffin cups, filling cups about halfway full.
5. Place cups in the air fryer basket, working in batches as necessary. Cook 15 minutes until muffins are brown at the edges and a toothpick inserted in the center comes out clean. Serve warm.

Breakfast Chimichangas

Servings: 4
Cooking Time: 8 Minutes
Ingredients:
- Four 8-inch flour tortillas
- ½ cup canned refried beans
- 1 cup scrambled eggs
- ½ cup grated cheddar or Monterey jack cheese
- 1 tablespoon vegetable oil
- 1 cup salsa

Directions:
1. Lay the flour tortillas out flat on a cutting board. In the center of each tortilla, spread 2 tablespoons refried beans. Next, add ¼ cup eggs and 2 tablespoons cheese to each tortilla.
2. To fold the tortillas, begin on the left side and fold to the center. Then fold the right side into the center. Next fold the bottom and top down and roll over to completely seal the chimichanga. Using a pastry brush or oil mister, brush the tops of the tortilla packages with oil.
3. Preheat the air fryer to 400°F (205°C) for 4 minutes. Place the chimichangas into the air fryer basket, seam side down, and air fry for 4 minutes. Using tongs, turn over the chimichangas and cook for an additional 2 to 3 minutes or until light golden brown.

Chocolate Chip Muffins

Servings: 6
Cooking Time: 15 Minutes
Ingredients:
- 1½ cups blanched finely ground almond flour
- ⅓ cup granular brown erythritol
- 4 tablespoons salted butter, melted
- 2 large eggs, whisked
- 1 tablespoon baking powder
- ½ cup low-carb chocolate chips

Directions:
1. In a large bowl, combine all ingredients. Evenly pour batter into six silicone muffin cups greased with cooking spray.
2. Place muffin cups into air fryer basket. Adjust the temperature to 320°F (160°C) and set the timer for 15 minutes. Muffins will be golden brown when done.
3. Let muffins cool in cups 15 minutes to avoid crumbling. Serve warm.

Fry Bread

Servings: 4
Cooking Time: 5 Minutes
Ingredients:
- 1 cup flour
- 2 teaspoons baking powder
- ¼ teaspoon salt
- ¼ cup lukewarm milk
- 1 teaspoon oil
- 2–3 tablespoons water
- oil for misting or cooking spray

Directions:
1. Stir together flour, baking powder, and salt. Gently mix in the milk and oil. Stir in 1 tablespoon water. If needed, add more water 1 tablespoon at a time until stiff dough forms. Dough shouldn't be sticky, so use only as much as you need.
2. Divide dough into 4 portions and shape into balls. Cover with a towel and let rest for 10 minutes.
3. Preheat air fryer to 390°F (200°C).
4. Shape dough as desired:

5. a. Pat into 3-inch circles. This will make a thicker bread to eat plain or with a sprinkle of cinnamon or honey butter. You can cook all 4 at once.
6. b. Pat thinner into rectangles about 3 x 6 inches. This will create a thinner bread to serve as a base for dishes such as Indian tacos. The circular shape is more traditional, but rectangles allow you to cook 2 at a time in your air fryer basket.
7. Spray both sides of dough pieces with oil or cooking spray.
8. Place the 4 circles or 2 of the dough rectangles in the air fryer basket and cook at 390°F (200°C) for 3minutes. Spray tops, turn, spray other side, and cook for 2 more minutes. If necessary, repeat to cook remaining bread.
9. Serve piping hot as is or allow to cool slightly and add toppings to create your own Native American tacos.

Green Scramble

Servings: 4
Cooking Time: 20 Minutes
Ingredients:
- 1 tablespoon olive oil
- ½ teaspoon smoked paprika
- 12 eggs, whisked
- 3 cups baby spinach
- Salt and black pepper to the taste

Directions:
1. In a bowl, mix all the ingredients except the oil and whisk them well. Heat up your air fryer at 360°F (180°C), add the oil, heat it up, add the eggs and spinach mix, cover, cook for 20 minutes, divide between plates and serve.

Chives Omelet

Servings: 4
Cooking Time: 20 Minutes
Ingredients:
- 6 eggs, whisked
- 1 cup chives, chopped
- Cooking spray
- 1 cup mozzarella, shredded
- Salt and black pepper to the taste

Directions:
1. In a bowl, mix all the ingredients except the cooking spray and whisk well. Grease a pan that fits your air fryer with the cooking spray, pour the eggs mix, spread, put the pan into the machine and cook at 350°F (175°C) for 20 minutes. Divide the omelet between plates and serve for breakfast.

Hole In One

Servings: 1
Cooking Time: 7 Minutes
Ingredients:
- 1 slice bread
- 1 teaspoon soft butter
- 1 egg
- salt and pepper
- 1 tablespoon shredded Cheddar cheese
- 2 teaspoons diced ham

Directions:
1. Place a 6 x 6-inch baking dish inside air fryer basket and preheat fryer to 330°F (165°C).
2. Using a 2½-inch-diameter biscuit cutter, cut a hole in center of bread slice.
3. Spread softened butter on both sides of bread.
4. Lay bread slice in baking dish and crack egg into the hole. Sprinkle egg with salt and pepper to taste.
5. Cook for 5minutes.
6. Turn toast over and top it with shredded cheese and diced ham.
7. Cook for 2 more minutes or until yolk is done to your liking.

Egg Muffins

Servings: 4
Cooking Time: 11 Minutes
Ingredients:
- 4 eggs
- salt and pepper
- olive oil
- 4 English muffins, split
- 1 cup shredded Colby Jack cheese
- 4 slices ham or Canadian bacon

Directions:
1. Preheat air fryer to 390°F (200°C).
2. Beat together eggs and add salt and pepper to taste. Spray air fryer baking pan lightly with oil and add eggs. Cook for 2minutes, stir, and continue cooking for 4minutes, stirring every minute, until eggs are scrambled to your preference. Remove pan from air fryer.
3. Place bottom halves of English muffins in air fryer basket. Take half of the shredded cheese and divide it among the muffins. Top each with a slice of ham and one-quarter of the eggs. Sprinkle remaining cheese on top of the eggs. Use a fork to press the cheese into the egg a little so it doesn't slip off before it melts.
4. Cook at 360°F (180°C) for 1 minute. Add English muffin tops and cook for 4minutes to heat through and toast the muffins.

Mini Bacon Egg Quiches

Servings:6
Cooking Time: 30 Minutes
Ingredients:
- 3 eggs
- 2 tbsp heavy cream
- ¼ tsp Dijon mustard
- Salt and pepper to taste
- 3 oz cooked bacon, crumbled
- ¼ cup grated cheddar

Directions:
1. Preheat air fryer to 350ºF. Beat the eggs with salt and pepper in a bowl until fluffy. Stir in heavy cream, mustard, cooked bacon, and cheese. Divide the mixture between 6 greased muffin cups and place them in the frying basket. Bake for 8-10 minutes. Let cool slightly before serving.

Perfect Burgers

Servings: 3
Cooking Time: 13 Minutes
Ingredients:
- 1 pound 2 ounces 90% lean ground beef
- 1½ tablespoons Worcestershire sauce (gluten-free, if a concern)
- ½ teaspoon Ground black pepper
- 3 Hamburger buns (gluten-free if a concern), split open

Directions:
1. Preheat the air fryer to 375°F (190°C).
2. Gently mix the ground beef, Worcestershire sauce, and pepper in a bowl until well combined but preserving as much of the meat's fibers as possible. Divide this mixture into two 5-inch patties for the small batch, three 5-inch patties for the medium, or four 5-inch patties for the large. Make a thumbprint indentation in the center of each patty, about halfway through the meat.
3. Set the patties in the basket in one layer with some space between them. Air-fry undisturbed for 10 minutes, or until an instant-read meat thermometer inserted into the center of a burger registers 160°F (70°C). You may need to add 2 minutes cooking time if the air fryer is at 360°F (180°C).
4. Use a nonstick-safe spatula, and perhaps a flatware fork for balance, to transfer the burgers to a cutting board. Set the buns cut side down in the basket in one layer and air-fry undisturbed for 1 minute, to toast a bit and warm up. Serve the burgers in the warm buns.

Thai Turkey Sausage Patties

Servings: 4
Cooking Time: 30 Minutes
Ingredients:
- 12 oz turkey sausage
- 1 tsp onion powder
- 1 tsp dried coriander
- ¼ tsp Thai curry paste
- ¼ tsp red pepper flakes
- Salt and pepper to taste

Directions:
1. Preheat air fryer to 350°F (175°C). Place the sausage, onion, coriander, curry paste, red flakes, salt, and black pepper in a large bowl and mix well. Form into eight patties. Arrange the patties on the greased frying basket and Air Fry for 10 minutes, flipping once halfway through. Once the patties are cooked, transfer to a plate and serve hot.

Bacon Puff Pastry Pinwheels

Servings: 8
Cooking Time: 10 Minutes
Ingredients:
- 1 sheet of puff pastry
- 2 tablespoons maple syrup
- ¼ cup brown sugar
- 8 slices bacon (not thick cut)
- coarsely cracked black pepper
- vegetable oil

Directions:
1. On a lightly floured surface, roll the puff pastry out into a square that measures roughly 10 inches wide by however long your bacon strips are. Cut the pastry into eight even strips.
2. Brush the strips of pastry with the maple syrup and sprinkle the brown sugar on top, leaving 1 inch of dough exposed at the far end of each strip. Place a slice of bacon on each strip of puff pastry, letting 1/8-inch of the length of bacon hang over the edge of the pastry. Season generously with coarsely ground black pepper.
3. With the exposed end of the pastry strips away from you, roll the bacon and pastry strips up into pinwheels. Dab a little water on the exposed end of the pastry and pinch it to the pinwheel to seal the pastry shut.
4. Preheat the air fryer to 360°F (180°C).
5. Brush or spray the air fryer basket with a little vegetable oil. Place the pinwheels into the basket and air-fry at 360°F (180°C) for 8 minutes. Turn the pinwheels over and air-fry for another 2 minutes to brown the bottom. Serve warm.

Creamy Parsley Soufflé

Servings: 2
Cooking Time: 10 Minutes
Ingredients:
- 2 eggs
- 1 tablespoon fresh parsley, chopped
- 1 fresh red chili pepper, chopped
- 2 tablespoons light cream
- Salt, to taste

Directions:
1. Preheat the Air fryer to 390°F (200C) and grease 2 soufflé dishes.
2. Mix together all the ingredients in a bowl until well combined.
3. Transfer the mixture into prepared soufflé dishes and place in the Air fryer.
4. Cook for about 10 minutes and dish out to serve warm.

Jalapeño Egg Cups

Servings: 4
Cooking Time: 14 Minutes
Ingredients:
- 4 large eggs
- ½ teaspoon salt
- ¼ teaspoon ground black pepper
- ¼ cup chopped pickled jalapeños
- 2 ounces cream cheese, softened
- ¼ teaspoon garlic powder
- ½ cup shredded sharp Cheddar cheese

Directions:
1. In a medium bowl, beat eggs together with salt and pepper, then pour evenly into four 4" ramekins greased with cooking spray.

2. In a separate large bowl, mix jalapeños, cream cheese, garlic powder, and Cheddar. Spoon ¼ of the mixture into the center of one ramekin. Repeat with remaining mixture and ramekins.
3. Place ramekins in air fryer basket. Adjust the temperature to 320°F (160°C) and set the timer for 14 minutes. Eggs will be set when done. Serve warm.

Simple Egg Soufflé

Servings: 2
Cooking Time: 8 Minutes
Ingredients:
- 2 eggs
- 1/4 tsp chili pepper
- 2 tbsp heavy cream
- 1/4 tsp pepper
- 1 tbsp parsley, chopped
- Salt

Directions:
1. In a bowl, whisk eggs with remaining gradients.
2. Spray two ramekins with cooking spray.
3. Pour egg mixture into the prepared ramekins and place into the air fryer basket.
4. Cook soufflé at 390°F (200°C) for 8 minutes.
5. Serve and enjoy.

Medium Rare Simple Salt And Pepper Steak

Servings: 3
Cooking Time: 30 Minutes
Ingredients:
- 1 ½ pounds skirt steak
- Salt and pepper to taste

Directions:
1. Preheat the air fryer at 390°F (200°C).
2. Place the grill pan accessory in the air fryer.
3. Season the skirt steak with salt and pepper.
4. Place on the grill pan and cook for 15 minutes per batch.
5. Flip the meat halfway through the cooking time.

Grilled Bbq Sausages

Servings: 3
Cooking Time: 30 Minutes
Ingredients:
- 6 sausage links
- ½ cup prepared BBQ sauce

Directions:
1. Preheat the air fryer at 390°F (200°C).
2. Place the grill pan accessory in the air fryer.
3. Place the sausage links and grill for 30 minutes.
4. Flip halfway through the cooking time.
5. Before serving brush with prepared BBQ sauce.

Bunless Breakfast Turkey Burgers

Servings: 4
Cooking Time: 15 Minutes
Ingredients:
- 1 pound ground turkey breakfast sausage
- ½ teaspoon salt
- ¼ teaspoon ground black pepper
- ¼ cup seeded and chopped green bell pepper
- 2 tablespoons mayonnaise
- 1 medium avocado, peeled, pitted, and sliced

Directions:
1. In a large bowl, mix sausage with salt, black pepper, bell pepper, and mayonnaise. Form meat into four patties.
2. Place patties into ungreased air fryer basket. Adjust the temperature to 370°F (185°C) and set the timer for 15 minutes, turning patties halfway through cooking. Burgers will be done when dark brown and they have an internal temperature of at least 165°F (75°C).
3. Serve burgers topped with avocado slices on four medium plates.

Pigs In A Blanket

Servings: 10
Cooking Time: 8 Minutes
Ingredients:
- 1 cup all-purpose flour, plus more for rolling
- 1 teaspoon baking powder
- ¼ cup salted butter, cut into small pieces
- ½ cup buttermilk
- 10 fully cooked breakfast sausage links

Directions:
1. In a large mixing bowl, whisk together the flour and baking powder. Using your fingers or a pastry blender, cut in the butter until you have small pea-size crumbles.
2. Using a rubber spatula, make a well in the center of the flour mixture. Pour the buttermilk into the well, and fold the mixture together until you form a dough ball.
3. Place the sticky dough onto a floured surface and, using a floured rolling pin, roll out until ½-inch thick. Using a round biscuit cutter, cut out 10 rounds, reshaping the dough and rolling out, as needed.
4. Place 1 fully cooked breakfast sausage link on the left edge of each biscuit and roll up, leaving the ends slightly exposed.
5. Using a pastry brush, brush the biscuits with the whisked eggs, and spray them with cooking spray.
6. Place the pigs in a blanket into the air fryer basket with at least 1 inch between each biscuit. Set the air fryer to 340°F (170°C) and cook for 8 minutes.

Parsley Omelet

Servings: 4
Cooking Time: 15 Minutes
Ingredients:
- 4 eggs, whisked
- 1 tablespoon parsley, chopped
- ½ teaspoons cheddar cheese, shredded
- 1 avocado, peeled, pitted and cubed
- Cooking spray

Directions:
1. In a bowl, mix all the ingredients except the cooking spray and whisk well. Grease a baking pan that fits the Air Fryer with the cooking spray, pour the omelet mix, spread, introduce the pan in the machine and cook at 370°F (185°C) for 15 minutes. Serve for breakfast.

Cheesy Cauliflower "hash Browns"

Servings: 6
Cooking Time: 24 Minutes
Ingredients:
- 2 ounces 100% cheese crisps
- 1 steamer bag cauliflower, cooked according to package instructions
- 1 large egg
- ½ cup shredded sharp Cheddar cheese
- ½ teaspoon salt

Directions:
1. Let cooked cauliflower cool 10 minutes.
2. Place cheese crisps into food processor and pulse on low 30 seconds until crisps are finely ground.
3. Using a kitchen towel, wring out excess moisture from cauliflower and place into food processor.
4. Add egg to food processor and sprinkle with Cheddar and salt. Pulse five times until mixture is mostly smooth.
5. Cut two pieces of parchment to fit air fryer basket. Separate mixture into six even scoops and place three on each piece of ungreased parchment, keeping at least 2" of space between each scoop. Press each into a hash brown shape, about ¼" thick.
6. Place one batch on parchment into air fryer basket. Adjust the temperature to 375°F (190°C) and set the timer for 12 minutes, turning hash browns halfway through cooking. Hash browns will be golden brown when done. Repeat with second batch.
7. Allow 5 minutes to cool. Serve warm.

Spinach Spread

Servings: 4
Cooking Time: 10 Minutes
Ingredients:
- 2 tablespoons coconut cream
- 3 cups spinach leaves
- 2 tablespoons cilantro
- 2 tablespoons bacon, cooked and crumbled
- Salt and black pepper to the taste

Directions:
1. In a pan that fits the air fryer, combine all the ingredients except the bacon, put the pan in the machine and cook at 360°F (180°C) for 10 minutes. Transfer to a blender, pulse well, divide into bowls and serve with bacon sprinkled on top.

Smoked Salmon Croissant Sandwich

Servings: 1
Cooking Time: 30 Minutes
Ingredients:
- 1 croissant, halved
- 2 eggs
- 1 tbsp guacamole
- 1 smoked salmon slice
- Salt and pepper to taste

Directions:
1. Preheat air fryer to 360°F (180°C). Place the croissant, crusty side up, in the frying basket side by side. Whisk the eggs in a small ceramic dish until fluffy. Place in the air fryer. Bake for 10 minutes. Gently scramble the half-cooked egg in the baking dish with a fork. Flip the croissant and cook for another 10 minutes until the scrambled eggs are cooked, but still fluffy, and the croissant is toasted.
2. Place one croissant on a serving plate, then spread the guacamole on top. Scoop the scrambled eggs onto guacamole, then top with smoked salmon. Sprinkle with salt and pepper. Top with the second slice of toasted croissant, close sandwich, and serve hot.

Egg White Frittata

Servings: 2
Cooking Time: 8 Minutes
Ingredients:
- 2 cups liquid egg whites
- ½ cup chopped fresh spinach
- ¼ cup chopped Roma tomato
- ½ teaspoon salt
- ¼ cup chopped white onion

Directions:
1. Preheat the air fryer to 320°F (160°C). Spray a 6" round baking dish with cooking spray.
2. In a large bowl, whisk egg whites until frothy. Mix in spinach, tomato, salt, and onion. Stir until combined.
3. Pour egg mixture into prepared dish.
4. Place in the air fryer basket and cook 8 minutes until the center is set. Serve warm.

Strawberry Pastry

Servings: 8
Cooking Time: 15 Minutes Per Batch
Ingredients:
- 1 package refrigerated piecrust
- 1 cup strawberry jam
- 1 large egg, whisked
- ½ cup confectioners' sugar
- 2 tablespoons whole milk
- ½ teaspoon vanilla extract

Directions:
1. Preheat the air fryer to 320°F (160°C). Cut parchment paper to fit the air fryer basket.
2. On a lightly floured surface, lay piecrusts out flat. Cut each piecrust round into six 4" × 3" rectangles, reserving excess dough.
3. Form remaining dough into a ball, then roll out and cut four additional 4" × 3" rectangles, bringing the total to sixteen.
4. For each pastry, spread 2 tablespoons jam on a pastry rectangle, leaving a 1" border around the edges. Top with a second pastry rectangle and use a fork to gently press all four edges together. Repeat with remaining jam and pastry.
5. Brush tops of each pastry with egg and cut an X in the center of each to prevent excess steam from building up.
6. Place pastries on parchment in the air fryer basket, working in batches as necessary. Cook 12 minutes, then

Ninja Air Fryer Cookbook

carefully flip and cook an additional 3 minutes until each side is golden brown. Let cool 10 minutes.
7. In a small bowl, whisk confectioners' sugar, milk, and vanilla. Brush each pastry with glaze, then place in the refrigerator 5 minutes to set before serving.

Cinnamon Granola
Servings:4
Cooking Time: 7 Minutes
Ingredients:
- 2 cups shelled pecans, chopped
- 1 cup unsweetened coconut flakes
- 1 cup slivered almonds
- 2 tablespoons granular erythritol
- 1 teaspoon ground cinnamon

Directions:
1. In a large bowl, mix all ingredients. Place mixture into an ungreased 6" round nonstick baking dish.
2. Place dish into air fryer basket. Adjust the temperature to 320°F (160°C) and set the timer for 7 minutes, stirring halfway through cooking.
3. Let cool in dish 10 minutes before serving. Store in airtight container at room temperature up to 5 days.

Eggplant Parmesan Subs
Servings: 2
Cooking Time: 13 Minutes
Ingredients:
- 4 Peeled eggplant slices
- Olive oil spray
- 2 tablespoons plus 2 teaspoons Jarred pizza sauce, any variety except creamy
- ¼ cup (about ⅔ ounce) Finely grated Parmesan cheese
- 2 Small, long soft rolls, such as hero, hoagie, or Italian sub rolls (gluten-free, if a concern), split open lengthwise

Directions:
1. Preheat the air fryer to 350°F (175°C).
2. When the machine is at temperature, coat both sides of the eggplant slices with olive oil spray. Set them in the basket in one layer and air-fry undisturbed for 10 minutes, until lightly browned and softened.
3. Increase the machine's temperature to 375°F (190°C). Top each eggplant slice with 2 teaspoons pizza sauce, then 1 tablespoon cheese. Air-fry undisturbed for 2 minutes, or until the cheese has melted.
4. Use a nonstick-safe spatula, and perhaps a flatware fork for balance, to transfer the eggplant slices cheese side up to a cutting board. Set the roll(s) cut side down in the basket in one layer and air-fry undisturbed for 1 minute, to toast the rolls a bit and warm them up. Set 2 eggplant slices in each warm roll.

Jalapeño And Bacon Breakfast Pizza
Servings:2
Cooking Time: 10 Minutes
Ingredients:
- 1 cup shredded mozzarella cheese
- 1 ounce cream cheese, broken into small pieces
- 4 slices cooked sugar-free bacon, chopped
- ¼ cup chopped pickled jalapeños
- 1 large egg, whisked
- ¼ teaspoon salt

Directions:
1. Place mozzarella in a single layer on the bottom of an ungreased 6" round nonstick baking dish. Scatter cream cheese pieces, bacon, and jalapeños over mozzarella, then pour egg evenly around baking dish.
2. Sprinkle with salt and place into air fryer basket. Adjust the temperature to 330°F (165°C) and set the timer for 10 minutes. When cheese is brown and egg is set, pizza will be done.
3. Let cool on a large plate 5 minutes before serving.

Buttery Scallops
Servings: 2
Cooking Time: 8 Minutes
Ingredients:
- 1 lb jumbo scallops
- 1 tbsp fresh lemon juice
- 2 tbsp butter, melted

Directions:
1. Preheat the air fryer to 400°F (205°C).
2. In a small bowl, mix together lemon juice and butter.
3. Brush scallops with lemon juice and butter mixture and place into the air fryer basket.
4. Cook scallops for 4 minutes. Turn halfway through.
5. Again brush scallops with lemon butter mixture and cook for 4 minutes more. Turn halfway through.
6. Serve and enjoy.

Cream Cheese Danish
Servings:4
Cooking Time: 10 Minutes
Ingredients:
- 1 sheet frozen puff pastry dough, thawed
- 1 large egg, beaten
- 4 ounces full-fat cream cheese, softened
- ¼ cup confectioners' sugar
- 1 teaspoon vanilla extract
- ½ teaspoon lemon juice

Directions:
1. Preheat the air fryer to 320°F (160°C).
2. Unfold puff pastry and cut into four equal squares. For each pastry, fold all four corners partway to the center, leaving a 1" square in the center.
3. Brush egg evenly over folded puff pastry.
4. In a medium bowl, mix cream cheese, confectioners' sugar, vanilla, and lemon juice. Scoop 2 tablespoons of mixture into the center of each pastry square.
5. Place danishes directly in the air fryer basket and cook 10 minutes until puffy and golden brown. Cool 5 minutes before serving.

Easy Egg Bites

Servings: 2
Cooking Time: 9 Minutes
Ingredients:
- 2 large eggs
- ¼ cup full-fat cottage cheese
- ¼ cup shredded sharp Cheddar cheese
- ¼ teaspoon salt
- ⅛ teaspoon ground black pepper
- 6 tablespoons diced cooked ham

Directions:
1. Preheat the air fryer to 300°F (150°C). Spray six silicone muffin cups with cooking spray.
2. In a blender, place eggs, cottage cheese, Cheddar, salt, and pepper. Pulse five times until smooth and frothy.
3. Place 1 tablespoon ham in the bottom of each prepared baking cup, then divide egg mixture among cups.
4. Place in the air fryer basket and cook 9 minutes until egg bites are firm in the center. Carefully remove cups from air fryer basket and cool 3 minutes before serving. Serve warm.

Mini Tomato Quiche

Servings: 2
Cooking Time: 30 Minutes
Ingredients:
- 4 eggs
- ¼ cup onion, chopped
- ½ cup tomatoes, chopped
- ½ cup milk
- 1 cup Gouda cheese, shredded
- Salt, to taste

Directions:
1. Preheat the Air fryer to 340°F (170°C) and grease a large ramekin with cooking spray.
2. Mix together all the ingredients in a ramekin and transfer into the air fryer basket.
3. Cook for about 30 minutes and dish out to serve hot.

Banana Baked Oatmeal

Servings: 2
Cooking Time: 10 Minutes
Ingredients:
- 1 cup quick-cooking oats
- 1 cup whole milk
- 2 tablespoons unsalted butter, melted
- 1 medium banana, peeled and mashed
- 2 tablespoons brown sugar
- ½ teaspoon vanilla extract
- ½ teaspoon salt

Directions:
1. Preheat the air fryer to 360°F (180°C).
2. In a 6" round pan, add oats. Pour in milk and butter.
3. In a medium bowl, mix banana, brown sugar, vanilla, and salt until combined. Add to pan and mix until well combined.
4. Place in the air fryer and cook 10 minutes until the top is brown and oats feel firm to the touch. Serve warm.

Zucchini And Spring Onions Cakes

Servings: 4
Cooking Time: 8 Minutes
Ingredients:
- 8 ounces zucchinis, chopped
- 2 spring onions, chopped
- 2 eggs, whisked
- Salt and black pepper to the taste
- ¼ teaspoon sweet paprika, chopped
- Cooking spray

Directions:
1. In a bowl, mix all the ingredients except the cooking spray, stir well and shape medium fritters out of this mix. Put the basket in the Air Fryer, add the fritters inside, grease them with cooking spray and cook at 400°F (205°C) for 8 minutes. Divide the fritters between plates and serve for breakfast.

Egg White Cups

Servings: 4
Cooking Time: 15 Minutes
Ingredients:
- 2 cups 100% liquid egg whites
- 3 tablespoons salted butter, melted
- ¼ teaspoon salt
- ¼ teaspoon onion powder
- ½ medium Roma tomato, cored and diced
- ½ cup chopped fresh spinach leaves

Directions:
1. In a large bowl, whisk egg whites with butter, salt, and onion powder. Stir in tomato and spinach, then pour evenly into four 4" ramekins greased with cooking spray.
2. Place ramekins into air fryer basket. Adjust the temperature to 300°F (150°C) and set the timer for 15 minutes. Eggs will be fully cooked and firm in the center when done. Serve warm.

Roasted Golden Mini Potatoes

Servings: 4
Cooking Time: 22 Minutes
Ingredients:
- 6 cups water
- 1 pound baby Dutch yellow potatoes, quartered
- 2 tablespoons olive oil
- ½ teaspoon garlic powder
- ¾ teaspoon seasoned salt
- ¼ teaspoon salt
- ½ teaspoon ground black pepper

Directions:
1. In a medium saucepan over medium-high heat bring water to a boil. Add potatoes and boil 10 minutes until fork-tender, then drain and gently pat dry.
2. Preheat the air fryer to 400°F (205°C).
3. Drizzle oil over potatoes, then sprinkle with garlic powder, seasoned salt, salt, and pepper.
4. Place potatoes in the air fryer basket and cook 12 minutes, shaking the basket three times during cooking. Potatoes will be done when golden brown and edges are crisp. Serve warm.

Ninja Air Fryer Cookbook

Parmesan Garlic Naan

Servings: 6
Cooking Time: 4 Minutes
Ingredients:
- 1 cup bread flour
- 1 teaspoon baking powder
- ⅛ teaspoon salt
- 1 teaspoon garlic powder
- 2 tablespoon shredded parmesan cheese
- 1 cup plain 2% fat Greek yogurt
- 1 tablespoon extra-virgin olive oil

Directions:
1. Preheat the air fryer to 400°F (205°C).
2. In a medium bowl, mix the flour, baking powder, salt, garlic powder, and cheese. Mix the yogurt into the flour, using your hands to combine if necessary.
3. On a flat surface covered with flour, divide the dough into 6 equal balls and roll each out into a 4-inch-diameter circle.
4. Lightly brush both sides of each naan with olive oil and place one naan at a time into the basket. Cook for 3 to 4 minutes. Remove and repeat for the remaining breads.
5. Serve warm.

Breakfast Quiche

Servings: 4
Cooking Time: 18 Minutes
Ingredients:
- 1 refrigerated piecrust
- 2 large eggs
- ¼ cup heavy cream
- ½ teaspoon salt
- ¼ teaspoon ground black pepper
- ½ cup shredded Cheddar cheese
- 2 slices bacon, cooked and crumbled

Directions:
1. Preheat the air fryer to 325°F (160°C). Spray a 6" pie pan with cooking spray. Trim piecrust to fit the pan.
2. In a medium bowl, whisk together eggs, cream, salt, and pepper. Stir in Cheddar and bacon.
3. Pour egg mixture into crust and cook 18 minutes until firm, brown, and a knife inserted into the center comes out clean. Serve warm.

Bacon, Egg, And Cheese Calzones

Servings: 4
Cooking Time: 12 Minutes
Ingredients:
- 2 large eggs
- 1 cup blanched finely ground almond flour
- 2 cups shredded mozzarella cheese
- 2 ounces cream cheese, softened and broken into small pieces
- 4 slices cooked sugar-free bacon, crumbled

Directions:
1. Beat eggs in a small bowl. Pour into a medium nonstick skillet over medium heat and scramble. Set aside.
2. In a large microwave-safe bowl, mix flour and mozzarella. Add cream cheese to bowl.
3. Place bowl in microwave and cook 45 seconds on high to melt cheese, then stir with a fork until a soft dough ball forms.
4. Cut a piece of parchment to fit air fryer basket. Separate dough into two sections and press each out into an 8" round.
5. On half of each dough round, place half of the scrambled eggs and crumbled bacon. Fold the other side of the dough over and press to seal the edges.
6. Place calzones on ungreased parchment and into air fryer basket. Adjust the temperature to 350°F (175°C) and set the timer for 12 minutes, turning calzones halfway through cooking. Crust will be golden and firm when done.
7. Let calzones cool on a cooking rack 5 minutes before serving.

Sweet Potato-cinnamon Toast

Servings: 6
Cooking Time: 8 Minutes
Ingredients:
- 1 small sweet potato, cut into ⅜-inch slices
- oil for misting
- ground cinnamon

Directions:
1. Preheat air fryer to 390°F (200°C).
2. Spray both sides of sweet potato slices with oil. Sprinkle both sides with cinnamon to taste.
3. Place potato slices in air fryer basket in a single layer.
4. Cook for 4 minutes, turn, and cook for 4 more minutes or until potato slices are barely fork tender.

Grilled Steak With Parsley Salad

Servings: 4
Cooking Time: 45 Minutes
Ingredients:
- 1 ½ pounds flatiron steak
- 3 tablespoons olive oil
- Salt and pepper to taste
- 2 cups parsley leaves
- ½ cup parmesan cheese, grated
- 1 tablespoon fresh lemon juice

Directions:
1. Preheat the air fryer at 390°F (200°C).
2. Place the grill pan accessory in the air fryer.
3. Mix together the steak, oil, salt and pepper.
4. Grill for 15 minutes per batch and make sure to flip the meat halfway through the cooking time.
5. Meanwhile, prepare the salad by combining in a bowl the parsley leaves, parmesan cheese and lemon juice. Season with salt and pepper.

Pancake For Two

Servings: 2
Cooking Time: 30 Minutes
Ingredients:
- 1 cup blanched finely ground almond flour
- 2 tablespoons granular erythritol
- 1 tablespoon salted butter, melted
- 1 large egg
- ⅓ cup unsweetened almond milk
- ½ teaspoon vanilla extract

Directions:
1. In a large bowl, mix all ingredients together, then pour half the batter into an ungreased 6" round nonstick baking dish.
2. Place dish into air fryer basket. Adjust the temperature to 320°F (160°C) and set the timer for 15 minutes. The pancake will be golden brown on top and firm, and a toothpick inserted in the center will come out clean when done. Repeat with remaining batter.
3. Slice in half in dish and serve warm.

Inside-out Cheeseburgers

Servings: 3
Cooking Time: 9-11 Minutes
Ingredients:
- 1 pound 2 ounces 90% lean ground beef
- ¾ teaspoon Dried oregano
- ¾ teaspoon Table salt
- ¾ teaspoon Ground black pepper
- ¼ teaspoon Garlic powder
- 6 tablespoons Shredded Cheddar, Swiss, or other semi-firm cheese, or a purchased blend of shredded cheeses
- 3 Hamburger buns (gluten-free, if a concern), split open

Directions:
1. Preheat the air fryer to 375°F (190°C).
2. Gently mix the ground beef, oregano, salt, pepper, and garlic powder in a bowl until well combined without turning the mixture to mush. Form it into two 6-inch patties for the small batch, three for the medium, or four for the large.
3. Place 2 tablespoons of the shredded cheese in the center of each patty. With clean hands, fold the sides of the patty up to cover the cheese, then pick it up and roll it gently into a ball to seal the cheese inside. Gently press it back into a 5-inch burger without letting any cheese squish out. Continue filling and preparing more burgers, as needed.
4. Place the burgers in the basket in one layer and air-fry undisturbed for 8 minutes for medium or 10 minutes for well-done.
5. Use a nonstick-safe spatula, and perhaps a flatware fork for balance, to transfer the burgers to a cutting board. Set the buns cut side down in the basket in one layer and air-fry undisturbed for 1 minute, to toast a bit and warm up. Cool the burgers a few minutes more, then serve them warm in the buns.

White Wheat Walnut Bread

Servings: 8
Cooking Time: 25 Minutes
Ingredients:
- 1 cup lukewarm water
- 1 packet RapidRise yeast
- 1 tablespoon light brown sugar
- 2 cups whole-grain white wheat flour
- 1 egg, room temperature, beaten with a fork
- 2 teaspoons olive oil
- ½ teaspoon salt
- ½ cup chopped walnuts
- cooking spray

Directions:
1. In a small bowl, mix the water, yeast, and brown sugar.
2. Pour yeast mixture over flour and mix until smooth.
3. Add the egg, olive oil, and salt and beat with a wooden spoon for 2 minutes.
4. Stir in chopped walnuts. You will have very thick batter rather than stiff bread dough.
5. Spray air fryer baking pan with cooking spray and pour in batter, smoothing the top.
6. Let batter rise for 15 minutes.
7. Preheat air fryer to 360°F (180°C).
8. Cook bread for 25 minutes, until toothpick pushed into center comes out with crumbs clinging. Let bread rest for 10 minutes before removing from pan.

Pizza Eggs

Servings: 2
Cooking Time: 10 Minutes
Ingredients:
- 1 cup shredded mozzarella cheese
- 7 slices pepperoni, chopped
- 1 large egg, whisked
- ¼ teaspoon dried oregano
- ¼ teaspoon dried parsley
- ¼ teaspoon garlic powder
- ¼ teaspoon salt

Directions:
1. Place mozzarella in a single layer on the bottom of an ungreased 6" round nonstick baking dish. Scatter pepperoni over cheese, then pour egg evenly around baking dish.
2. Sprinkle with remaining ingredients and place into air fryer basket. Adjust the temperature to 330°F (165°C) and set the timer for 10 minutes. When cheese is brown and egg is set, dish will be done.
3. Let cool in dish 5 minutes before serving.

Banana-nut Muffins

Servings: 12
Cooking Time: 15 Minutes
Ingredients:
- 1 ½ cups all-purpose flour
- ½ cup granulated sugar
- 1 teaspoon baking powder

- ½ cup salted butter, melted
- 1 large egg
- 2 medium bananas, peeled and mashed
- ½ cup chopped pecans

Directions:
1. Preheat the air fryer to 300°F (150°C).
2. In a large bowl, whisk together flour, sugar, and baking powder.
3. Add butter, egg, and bananas to dry mixture. Stir until well combined. Batter will be thick.
4. Gently fold in pecans. Divide batter evenly among twelve silicone or aluminum muffin cups, filling cups about halfway full.
5. Place cups in the air fryer basket, working in batches as necessary. Cook 15 minutes until muffin edges are brown and a toothpick inserted into the center comes out clean. Let cool 5 minutes before serving.

All-in-one Breakfast Toast

Servings: 1
Cooking Time: 10 Minutes

Ingredients:
- 1 strip of bacon, diced
- 1 slice of 1-inch thick bread (such as Texas Toast or hand-sliced bread)
- 1 tablespoon softened butter (optional)
- 1 egg
- salt and freshly ground black pepper
- ¼ cup grated Colby or Jack cheese

Directions:
1. Preheat the air fryer to 400°F (205°C).
2. Air-fry the bacon for 3 minutes, shaking the basket once or twice while it cooks. Remove the bacon to a paper towel lined plate and set aside.
3. Use a sharp paring knife to score a large circle in the middle of the slice of bread, cutting halfway through, but not all the way through to the cutting board. Press down on the circle in the center of the bread slice to create an indentation. If using, spread the softened butter on the edges and in the hole of the bread.
4. Transfer the slice of bread, hole side up, to the air fryer basket. Crack the egg into the center of the bread, and season with salt and pepper.
5. Air-fry at 380°F (195°C) for 5 minutes. Sprinkle the grated cheese around the edges of the bread leaving the center of the yolk uncovered, and top with the cooked bacon. Press the cheese and bacon into the bread lightly to help anchor it to the bread and prevent it from blowing around in the air fryer.
6. Air-fry for one or two more minutes, just to melt the cheese and finish cooking the egg. Serve immediately.

Chapter 6: Vegetarians Recipes

Caprese Eggplant Stacks

Servings: 4
Cooking Time: 8 Minutes
Ingredients:
- 1 medium eggplant, cut into 4 (½") slices
- ½ teaspoon salt
- ¼ teaspoon ground black pepper
- 4 (¼") slices tomato
- 2 ounces fresh mozzarella cheese, cut into 4 slices
- 1 tablespoon olive oil
- ¼ cup fresh basil, sliced

Directions:
1. Preheat the air fryer to 320°F (160°C).
2. In a 6" round pan, place eggplant slices. Sprinkle with salt and pepper. Top each with a tomato slice, then a mozzarella slice, and drizzle with oil.
3. Place in the air fryer basket and cook 8 minutes until eggplant is tender and cheese is melted. Garnish with fresh basil to serve.

Spinach Pesto Flatbread

Servings: 4
Cooking Time: 8 Minutes Per Batch
Ingredients:
- 1 cup basil pesto
- 4 round flatbreads
- ½ cup chopped frozen spinach, thawed and drained
- 8 ounces fresh mozzarella cheese, sliced
- 1 teaspoon crushed red pepper flakes

Directions:
1. Preheat the air fryer to 350°F (175°C).
2. For each flatbread, spread ¼ cup pesto across flatbread, then scatter 2 tablespoons spinach over pesto. Top with 2 ounces mozzarella slices and ¼ teaspoon red pepper flakes. Repeat with remaining flatbread and toppings.
3. Place in the air fryer basket, working in batches as necessary, and cook 8 minutes until cheese is brown and bubbling. Serve warm.

Pizza Dough

Servings: 4
Cooking Time: 1 Hour 10 Minutes, Plus 10 Minutes For Additional Batches
Ingredients:
- 2 cups all-purpose flour
- 1 tablespoon granulated sugar
- 1 tablespoon quick-rise yeast
- 4 tablespoons olive oil, divided
- ¾ cup warm water

Directions:
1. In a large bowl, mix flour, sugar, and yeast until combined. Add 2 tablespoons oil and warm water and mix until dough becomes smooth.
2. On a lightly floured surface, knead dough 10 minutes, then form into a smooth ball. Drizzle with remaining 2 tablespoons oil, then cover with plastic. Let dough rise 1 hour until doubled in size.
3. Preheat the air fryer to 320°F (160°C).
4. Separate dough into four pieces and press each into a 6" pan or air fryer pizza tray that has been spritzed with cooking oil.
5. Add any desired toppings. Place in the air fryer basket, working in batches as necessary, and cook 10 minutes until crust is brown at the edges and toppings are heated through. Serve warm.

Tortilla Pizza Margherita

Servings: 1
Cooking Time: 15 Minutes
Ingredients:
- 1 flour tortilla
- ¼ cup tomato sauce
- 1/3 cup grated mozzarella
- 3 basil leaves

Directions:
1. Preheat air fryer to 350°F (175°C). Put the tortilla in the greased basket and pour the sauce in the center. Spread across the whole tortilla. Sprinkle with cheese and Bake for 8-10 minutes or until crisp. Remove carefully and top with basil leaves. Serve hot.

Pesto Vegetable Kebabs

Servings: 4
Cooking Time: 8 Minutes
Ingredients:
- 12 ounces button mushrooms
- 12 ounces cherry tomatoes
- 2 medium zucchini, cut into ¼" slices
- 1 medium red onion, peeled and cut into 1" cubes
- 1 cup pesto, divided
- ½ teaspoon salt
- ¼ teaspoon ground black pepper

Directions:
1. Soak eight 6" skewers in water 10 minutes to avoid burning. Preheat the air fryer to 350°F (175°C).
2. Place a mushroom on a skewer, followed by a tomato, zucchini slice, and red onion piece. Repeat to fill up the skewer, then follow the same pattern for remaining skewers.
3. Brush each skewer evenly using ½ cup pesto. Sprinkle kebabs with salt and pepper. Place in the air fryer basket and cook 10 minutes, turning halfway through cooking time, until vegetables are tender. Brush kebabs with remaining ½ cup pesto before serving.

Italian Seasoned Easy Pasta Chips

Servings: 2
Cooking Time: 10 Minutes
Ingredients:
- ½ teaspoon salt
- 1 ½ teaspoon Italian seasoning blend
- 1 tablespoon nutritional yeast
- 1 tablespoon olive oil
- 2 cups whole wheat bowtie pasta

Directions:
1. Place the baking dish accessory in the air fryer.
2. Give a good stir.
3. Close the air fryer and cook for 10 minutes at 390°F (200°C).

Ninja Air Fryer Cookbook

White Cheddar And Mushroom Soufflés

Servings: 4
Cooking Time: 12 Minutes
Ingredients:
- 3 large eggs, whites and yolks separated
- ½ cup sharp white Cheddar cheese
- 3 ounces cream cheese, softened
- ¼ teaspoon cream of tartar
- ¼ teaspoon salt
- ¼ teaspoon ground black pepper
- ½ cup cremini mushrooms, sliced

Directions:
1. In a large bowl, whip egg whites until stiff peaks form, about 2 minutes. In a separate large bowl, beat Cheddar, egg yolks, cream cheese, cream of tartar, salt, and pepper together until combined.
2. Fold egg whites into cheese mixture, being careful not to stir. Fold in mushrooms, then pour mixture evenly into four ungreased 4" ramekins.
3. Place ramekins into air fryer basket. Adjust the temperature to 350°F (175°C) and set the timer for 12 minutes. Eggs will be browned on the top and firm in the center when done. Serve warm.

Cauliflower Rice-stuffed Peppers

Servings: 4
Cooking Time: 15 Minutes
Ingredients:
- 2 cups uncooked cauliflower rice
- ¾ cup drained canned petite diced tomatoes
- 2 tablespoons olive oil
- 1 cup shredded mozzarella cheese
- ¼ teaspoon salt
- ¼ teaspoon ground black pepper
- 4 medium green bell peppers, tops removed, seeded

Directions:
1. In a large bowl, mix all ingredients except bell peppers. Scoop mixture evenly into peppers.
2. Place peppers into ungreased air fryer basket. Adjust the temperature to 350°F (175°C) and set the timer for 15 minutes. Peppers will be tender and cheese will be melted when done. Serve warm.

Zucchini Gratin

Servings: 2
Cooking Time: 15 Minutes
Ingredients:
- 5 oz. parmesan cheese, shredded
- 1 tbsp. coconut flour
- 1 tbsp. dried parsley
- 2 zucchinis
- 1 tsp. butter, melted

Directions:
1. Mix the parmesan and coconut flour together in a bowl, seasoning with parsley to taste.
2. Cut the zucchini in half lengthwise and chop the halves into four slices.
3. Pre-heat the fryer at 400°F (205°C).
4. Pour the melted butter over the zucchini and then dip the zucchini into the parmesan-flour mixture, coating it all over. Cook the zucchini in the fryer for thirteen minutes.

Cauliflower Pizza Crust

Servings: 2
Cooking Time: 7 Minutes
Ingredients:
- 1 steamer bag cauliflower, cooked according to package instructions
- ½ cup shredded sharp Cheddar cheese
- 1 large egg
- 2 tablespoons blanched finely ground almond flour
- 1 teaspoon Italian seasoning

Directions:
1. Let cooked cauliflower cool for 10 minutes. Using a kitchen towel, wring out excess moisture from cauliflower and place into food processor.
2. Add Cheddar, egg, flour, and Italian seasoning to processor and pulse ten times until cauliflower is smooth and all ingredients are combined.
3. Cut two pieces of parchment paper to fit air fryer basket. Divide cauliflower mixture into two equal portions and press each into a 6" round on ungreased parchment.
4. Place crusts on parchment into air fryer basket. Adjust the temperature to 360°F (180°C) and set the timer for 7 minutes, gently turning crusts halfway through cooking.
5. Store crusts in refrigerator in an airtight container up to 4 days or freeze between sheets of parchment in a sealable storage bag for up to 2 months.

Spinach And Artichoke-stuffed Peppers

Servings: 4
Cooking Time: 15 Minutes
Ingredients:
- 2 ounces cream cheese, softened
- ½ cup shredded mozzarella cheese
- ½ cup chopped fresh spinach leaves
- ¼ cup chopped canned artichoke hearts
- 2 medium green bell peppers, halved and seeded

Directions:
1. In a medium bowl, mix cream cheese, mozzarella, spinach, and artichokes. Spoon ¼ cheese mixture into each pepper half.
2. Place peppers into ungreased air fryer basket. Adjust the temperature to 320°F (160°C) and set the timer for 15 minutes. Peppers will be tender and cheese will be bubbling and brown when done. Serve warm.

Crispy Cabbage Steaks

Servings: 4
Cooking Time: 10 Minutes
Ingredients:
- 1 small head green cabbage, cored and cut into ½"-thick slices
- ¼ teaspoon salt
- ¼ teaspoon ground black pepper
- 2 tablespoons olive oil
- 1 clove garlic, peeled and finely minced
- ½ teaspoon dried thyme
- ½ teaspoon dried parsley

Directions:
1. Sprinkle each side of cabbage with salt and pepper, then place into ungreased air fryer basket, working in batches if needed.
2. Drizzle each side of cabbage with olive oil, then sprinkle with remaining ingredients on both sides. Adjust the temperature to 350°F (175°C) and set the timer for 10 minutes, turning "steaks" halfway through cooking. Cabbage will be browned at the edges and tender when done. Serve warm.

Crispy Shawarma Broccoli

Servings: 4
Cooking Time: 25 Minutes
Ingredients:
- 1 pound broccoli, steamed and drained
- 2 tablespoons canola oil
- 1 teaspoon cayenne pepper
- 1 teaspoon sea salt
- 1 tablespoon Shawarma spice blend

Directions:
1. Toss all ingredients in a mixing bowl.
2. Roast in the preheated Air Fryer at 380°F (195°C) for 10 minutes, shaking the basket halfway through the cooking time.
3. Work in batches. Bon appétit!

Buttered Broccoli

Servings: 4
Cooking Time: 7 Minutes
Ingredients:
- 4 cups fresh broccoli florets
- 2 tablespoons butter, melted
- ¼ cup water
- Salt and black pepper, to taste

Directions:
1. Preheat the Air fryer to 400°F (205°C) and grease an Air fryer basket.
2. Mix broccoli, butter, salt, and black pepper in a bowl and toss to coat well.
3. Place water at the bottom of Air fryer pan and arrange the broccoli florets into the Air fryer basket.
4. Cook for about 7 minutes and dish out in a bowl to serve hot.

Garlic Okra Chips

Servings: 4
Cooking Time: 20 Minutes
Ingredients:
- 2 cups okra, cut into rounds
- 1 ½ tbsp. melted butter
- 1 garlic clove, minced
- 1 tsp powdered paprika
- Salt and pepper to taste

Directions:
1. Preheat air fryer to 350°F (175°C). Toss okra, melted butter, paprika, garlic, salt and pepper in a medium bowl until okra is coated. Place okra in the frying basket and Air Fry for 5 minutes. Shake the basket and Air Fry for another 5 minutes. Shake one more time and Air Fry for 2 minutes until crispy. Serve warm and enjoy.

Easy Glazed Carrots

Servings: 4
Cooking Time: 12 Minutes
Ingredients:
- 3 cups carrots, peeled and cut into large chunks
- 1 tablespoon olive oil
- 1 tablespoon honey
- Salt and black pepper, to taste

Directions:
1. Preheat the Air fryer to 390°F (200°C) and grease an Air fryer basket.
2. Mix all the ingredients in a bowl and toss to coat well.
3. Transfer into the Air fryer basket and cook for about 12 minutes.
4. Dish out and serve hot.

Crispy Wings With Lemony Old Bay Spice

Servings: 4
Cooking Time: 25 Minutes
Ingredients:
- ½ cup butter
- ¾ cup almond flour
- 1 tablespoon old bay spices
- 1 teaspoon lemon juice, freshly squeezed
- 3 pounds chicken wings
- Salt and pepper to taste

Directions:
1. Preheat the air fryer for 5 minutes.
2. In a mixing bowl, combine all ingredients except for the butter.
3. Place in the air fryer basket.
4. Cook for 25 minutes at 350°F (175°C).
5. Halfway through the cooking time, shake the fryer basket for even cooking.
6. Once cooked, drizzle with melted butter.

Sweet And Sour Brussel Sprouts
Servings: 2
Cooking Time: 10 Minutes
Ingredients:
- 2 cups Brussels sprouts, trimmed and halved lengthwise
- 1 tablespoon balsamic vinegar
- 1 tablespoon maple syrup
- Salt, as required

Directions:
1. Preheat the Air fryer to 400°F (205°C) and grease an Air fryer basket.
2. Mix all the ingredients in a bowl and toss to coat well.
3. Arrange the Brussel sprouts in the Air fryer basket and cook for about 10 minutes, shaking once halfway through.
4. Dish out in a bowl and serve hot.

Thyme Lentil Patties
Servings: 2
Cooking Time: 35 Minutes
Ingredients:
- ½ cup grated American cheese
- 1 cup cooked lentils
- ¼ tsp dried thyme
- 2 eggs, beaten
- Salt and pepper to taste
- 1 cup bread crumbs

Directions:
1. Preheat air fryer to 350°F (175°C). Put the eggs, lentils, and cheese in a bowl and mix to combine. Stir in half the bread crumbs, thyme, salt, and pepper. Form the mixture into 2 patties and coat them in the remaining bread crumbs. Transfer to the greased frying basket. Air Fry for 14-16 minutes until brown, flipping once. Serve.

Tacos
Servings: 24
Cooking Time: 8 Minutes Per Batch
Ingredients:
- 1 24-count package 4-inch corn tortillas
- 1½ cups refried beans
- 4 ounces sharp Cheddar cheese, grated
- ½ cup salsa
- oil for misting or cooking spray

Directions:
1. Preheat air fryer to 390°F (200°C).
2. Wrap refrigerated tortillas in damp paper towels and microwave for 30 to 60 seconds to warm. If necessary, rewarm tortillas as you go to keep them soft enough to fold without breaking.
3. Working with one tortilla at a time, top with 1 tablespoon of beans, 1 tablespoon of grated cheese, and 1 teaspoon of salsa. Fold over and press down very gently on the center. Press edges firmly all around to seal. Spray both sides with oil or cooking spray.
4. Cooking in two batches, place half the tacos in the air fryer basket. To cook 12 at a time, you may need to stand them upright and lean some against the sides of basket. It's okay if they're crowded as long as you leave a little room for air to circulate around them.
5. Cook for 8 minutes or until golden brown and crispy.
6. Repeat steps 4 and 5 to cook remaining tacos.

Breadcrumbs Stuffed Mushrooms
Servings: 4
Cooking Time: 10 Minutes
Ingredients:
- 1½ spelt bread slices
- 1 tablespoon flat-leaf parsley, finely chopped
- 16 small button mushrooms, stemmed and gills removed
- 1½ tablespoons olive oil
- 1 garlic clove, crushed
- Salt and black pepper, to taste

Directions:
1. Preheat the Air fryer to 390°F (200°C) and grease an Air fryer basket.
2. Put the bread slices in a food processor and pulse until fine crumbs form.
3. Transfer the crumbs into a bowl and stir in the olive oil, garlic, parsley, salt, and black pepper.
4. Stuff the breadcrumbs mixture in each mushroom cap and arrange the mushrooms in the Air fryer basket.
5. Cook for about 10 minutes and dish out in a bowl to serve warm.

Sweet And Spicy Barbecue Tofu
Servings: 4
Cooking Time: 1 Hour 15 Minutes
Ingredients:
- 1 package extra-firm tofu, drained
- ½ cup barbecue sauce
- ½ cup brown sugar
- 1 teaspoon liquid smoke
- 1 teaspoon crushed red pepper flakes
- ½ teaspoon salt
- Cooking spray

Directions:
1. Press tofu block to remove excess moisture. If you don't have a tofu press, line a baking sheet with paper towels and set tofu on top. Set a second baking sheet on top of tofu and weight it with a heavy item such as a skillet. Let tofu sit at least 30 minutes, changing paper towels if necessary.
2. Cut pressed tofu into twenty-four equal pieces. Set aside.
3. In a large bowl, combine barbecue sauce, brown sugar, liquid smoke, red pepper flakes, and salt. Mix well and add tofu, coating completely. Cover and let marinate at least 30 minutes on the counter.
4. Preheat the air fryer to 400°F (205°C).
5. Spray the air fryer basket with cooking spray and add marinated tofu. Cook 15 minutes, shaking the basket twice during cooking.
6. Let cool 10 minutes before serving warm.

Sautéed Spinach

Servings: 2
Cooking Time: 9 Minutes
Ingredients:
- 1 small onion, chopped
- 6 ounces fresh spinach
- 2 tablespoons olive oil
- 1 teaspoon ginger, minced
- Salt and black pepper, to taste

Directions:
1. Preheat the Air fryer to 360°F (180°C) and grease an Air fryer pan.
2. Put olive oil, onions and ginger in the Air fryer pan and place in the Air fryer basket.
3. Cook for about 4 minutes and add spinach, salt, and black pepper.
4. Cook for about 4 more minutes and dish out in a bowl to serve.

Sweet Pepper Nachos

Servings: 2
Cooking Time: 5 Minutes
Ingredients:
- 6 mini sweet peppers, seeded and sliced in half
- ¾ cup shredded Colby jack cheese
- ¼ cup sliced pickled jalapeños
- ½ medium avocado, peeled, pitted, and diced
- 2 tablespoons sour cream

Directions:
1. Place peppers into an ungreased 6" round nonstick baking dish. Sprinkle with Colby and top with jalapeños.
2. Place dish into air fryer basket. Adjust the temperature to 350°F (175°C) and set the timer for 5 minutes. Cheese will be melted and bubbly when done.
3. Remove dish from air fryer and top with avocado. Drizzle with sour cream. Serve warm.

Healthy Apple-licious Chips

Servings: 1
Cooking Time: 6 Minutes
Ingredients:
- ½ teaspoon ground cumin
- 1 apple, cored and sliced thinly
- 1 tablespoon sugar
- A pinch of salt

Directions:
1. Place all ingredients in a bowl and toss to coat everything.
2. Put the grill pan accessory in the air fryer and place the sliced apples on the grill pan.
3. Close the air fryer and cook for 6 minutes at 390°F (200°C).

Caramelized Brussels Sprout

Servings: 4
Cooking Time: 35 Minutes
Ingredients:
- 1 pound Brussels sprouts, trimmed and halved
- 4 teaspoons butter, melted
- Salt and black pepper, to taste

Directions:
1. Preheat the Air fryer to 400°F (205°C) and grease an Air fryer basket.
2. Mix all the ingredients in a bowl and toss to coat well.
3. Arrange the Brussels sprouts in the Air fryer basket and cook for about 35 minutes.
4. Dish out and serve warm.

Spicy Roasted Cashew Nuts

Servings: 4
Cooking Time: 20 Minutes
Ingredients:
- 1 cup whole cashews
- 1 teaspoon olive oil
- Salt and ground black pepper, to taste
- 1/2 teaspoon smoked paprika
- 1/2 teaspoon ancho chili powder

Directions:
1. Toss all ingredients in the mixing bowl.
2. Line the Air Fryer basket with baking parchment. Spread out the spiced cashews in a single layer in the basket.
3. Roast at 350°F (175°C) for 6 to 8 minutes, shaking the basket once or twice. Work in batches. Enjoy!

Pepper-pineapple With Butter-sugar Glaze

Servings: 2
Cooking Time: 10 Minutes
Ingredients:
- 1 medium-sized pineapple, peeled and sliced
- 1 red bell pepper, seeded and julienned
- 1 teaspoon brown sugar
- 2 teaspoons melted butter
- Salt to taste

Directions:
1. Preheat the air fryer to 390°F (200°C).
2. Place the grill pan accessory in the air fryer.
3. Mix all ingredients in a Ziploc bag and give a good shake.
4. Dump onto the grill pan and cook for 10 minutes making sure that you flip the pineapples every 5 minutes.

Stuffed Portobellos

Servings: 4
Cooking Time: 8 Minutes
Ingredients:
- 3 ounces cream cheese, softened
- ½ medium zucchini, trimmed and chopped
- ¼ cup seeded and chopped red bell pepper
- 1½ cups chopped fresh spinach leaves

- 4 large portobello mushrooms, stems removed
- 2 tablespoons coconut oil, melted
- ½ teaspoon salt

Directions:
1. In a medium bowl, mix cream cheese, zucchini, pepper, and spinach.
2. Drizzle mushrooms with coconut oil and sprinkle with salt. Scoop ¼ zucchini mixture into each mushroom.
3. Place mushrooms into ungreased air fryer basket. Adjust the temperature to 400°F (205°C) and set the timer for 8 minutes. Portobellos will be tender and tops will be browned when done. Serve warm.

Easy Baked Root Veggies

Servings: 4
Cooking Time: 45 Minutes
Ingredients:
- ¼ cup olive oil
- 1 head broccoli, cut into florets
- 1 tablespoon dry onion powder
- 2 sweet potatoes, peeled and cubed
- 4 carrots, cut into chunks
- 4 zucchinis, sliced thickly
- salt and pepper to taste

Directions:
1. Preheat the air fryer to 400°F (205°C).
2. In a baking dish that can fit inside the air fryer, mix all the ingredients and bake for 45 minutes or until the vegetables are tender and the sides have browned.

Eggplant Parmesan

Servings: 4
Cooking Time: 17 Minutes
Ingredients:
- 1 medium eggplant, ends trimmed, sliced into ½" rounds
- ¼ teaspoon salt
- 2 tablespoons coconut oil
- ½ cup grated Parmesan cheese
- 1 ounce 100% cheese crisps, finely crushed
- ½ cup low-carb marinara sauce
- ½ cup shredded mozzarella cheese

Directions:
1. Sprinkle eggplant rounds with salt on both sides and wrap in a kitchen towel for 30 minutes. Press to remove excess water, then drizzle rounds with coconut oil on both sides.
2. In a medium bowl, mix Parmesan and cheese crisps. Press each eggplant slice into mixture to coat both sides.
3. Place rounds into ungreased air fryer basket. Adjust the temperature to 350°F (175°C) and set the timer for 15 minutes, turning rounds halfway through cooking. They will be crispy around the edges when done.
4. When timer beeps, spoon marinara over rounds and sprinkle with mozzarella. Continue cooking an additional 2 minutes at 350°F (175°C) until cheese is melted. Serve warm.

Roasted Vegetable Pita Pizza

Servings: 4
Cooking Time: 20 Minutes
Ingredients:
- 1 medium red bell pepper, seeded and cut into quarters
- 1 teaspoon extra-virgin olive oil
- ⅛ teaspoon black pepper
- ⅛ teaspoon salt
- Two 6-inch whole-grain pita breads
- 6 tablespoons pesto sauce
- ¼ small red onion, thinly sliced
- ½ cup shredded part-skim mozzarella cheese

Directions:
1. Preheat the air fryer to 400°F (205°C).
2. In a small bowl, toss the bell peppers with the olive oil, pepper, and salt.
3. Place the bell peppers in the air fryer and cook for 15 minutes, shaking every 5 minutes to prevent burning.
4. Remove the peppers and set aside. Turn the air fryer temperature down to 350°F (175°C).
5. Lay the pita bread on a flat surface. Cover each with half the pesto sauce; then top with even portions of the red bell peppers and onions. Sprinkle cheese over the top. Spray the air fryer basket with olive oil mist.
6. Carefully lift the pita bread into the air fryer basket with a spatula.
7. Cook for 5 to 8 minutes, or until the outer edges begin to brown and the cheese is melted.
8. Serve warm with desired sides.

Zucchini Topped With Coconut Cream 'n Bacon

Servings: 3
Cooking Time: 20 Minutes
Ingredients:
- 1 tablespoon lemon juice
- 3 slices bacon, fried and crumbled
- 3 tablespoons olive oil
- 3 zucchini squashes
- 4 tablespoons coconut cream
- Salt and pepper to taste

Directions:
1. Preheat the air fryer for 5 minutes.
2. Line up chopsticks on both sides of the zucchini and slice thinly until you hit the stick. Brush the zucchinis with olive oil. Set aside.
3. Place the zucchini in the air fryer. Bake for 20 minutes at 350°F (175°C).
4. Meanwhile, combine the coconut cream and lemon juice in a mixing bowl. Season with salt and pepper to taste.
5. Once the zucchini is cooked, scoop the coconut cream mixture and drizzle on top.
6. Sprinkle with bacon bits.

Ninja Air Fryer Cookbook

Mediterranean Pan Pizza

Servings: 2
Cooking Time: 8 Minutes
Ingredients:
- 1 cup shredded mozzarella cheese
- ¼ medium red bell pepper, seeded and chopped
- ½ cup chopped fresh spinach leaves
- 2 tablespoons chopped black olives
- 2 tablespoons crumbled feta cheese

Directions:
1. Sprinkle mozzarella into an ungreased 6" round nonstick baking dish in an even layer. Add remaining ingredients on top.
2. Place dish into air fryer basket. Adjust the temperature to 350°F (175°C) and set the timer for 8 minutes, checking halfway through to avoid burning. Top of pizza will be golden brown and the cheese melted when done.
3. Remove dish from fryer and let cool 5 minutes before slicing and serving.

Two-cheese Grilled Sandwiches

Servings: 2
Cooking Time: 30 Minutes
Ingredients:
- 4 sourdough bread slices
- 2 cheddar cheese slices
- 2 Swiss cheese slices
- 1 tbsp butter
- 2 dill pickles, sliced

Directions:
1. Preheat air fryer to 360°F (180°C). Smear both sides of the sourdough bread with butter and place them in the frying basket. Toast the bread for 6 minutes, flipping once.
2. Divide the cheddar cheese between 2 of the bread slices. Cover the remaining 2 bread slices with Swiss cheese slices. Bake for 10 more minutes until the cheeses have melted and lightly bubbled and the bread has golden brown. Set the cheddar-covered bread slices on a serving plate, cover with pickles, and top each with the Swiss-covered slices. Serve and enjoy!

Turmeric Crispy Chickpeas

Servings: 4
Cooking Time: 22 Minutes
Ingredients:
- 1 tbsp butter, melted
- ½ tsp dried rosemary
- ¼ tsp turmeric
- Salt to taste

Directions:
1. Preheat the Air fryer to 380°F (195°C).
2. In a bowl, combine together chickpeas, butter, rosemary, turmeric, and salt; toss to coat. Place the prepared chickpeas in your Air Fryer's cooking basket and cook for 6 minutes. Slide out the basket and shake; cook for another 6 minutes until crispy.

Cauliflower Steaks Gratin

Servings: 2
Cooking Time: 13 Minutes
Ingredients:
- 1 head cauliflower
- 1 tablespoon olive oil
- salt and freshly ground black pepper
- ½ teaspoon chopped fresh thyme leaves
- 3 tablespoons grated Parmigiano-Reggiano cheese
- 2 tablespoons panko breadcrumbs

Directions:
1. Preheat the air-fryer to 370°F (185°C).
2. Cut two steaks out of the center of the cauliflower. To do this, cut the cauliflower in half and then cut one slice about 1-inch thick off each half. The rest of the cauliflower will fall apart into florets, which you can roast on their own or save for another meal.
3. Brush both sides of the cauliflower steaks with olive oil and season with salt, freshly ground black pepper and fresh thyme. Place the cauliflower steaks into the air fryer basket and air-fry for 6 minutes. Turn the steaks over and air-fry for another 4 minutes. Combine the Parmesan cheese and panko breadcrumbs and sprinkle the mixture over the tops of both steaks and air-fry for another 3 minutes until the cheese has melted and the breadcrumbs have browned. Serve this with some sautéed bitter greens and air-fried blistered tomatoes.

Spinach And Feta Pinwheels

Servings: 4
Cooking Time: 15 Minutes
Ingredients:
- 1 sheet frozen puff pastry, thawed
- 3 ounces full-fat cream cheese, softened
- 1 bag frozen spinach, thawed and drained
- ¼ teaspoon salt
- ⅓ cup crumbled feta cheese
- 1 large egg, whisked

Directions:
1. Preheat the air fryer to 320°F (160°C). Unroll puff pastry into a flat rectangle.
2. In a medium bowl, mix cream cheese, spinach, and salt until well combined.
3. Spoon cream cheese mixture onto pastry in an even layer, leaving a ½" border around the edges.
4. Sprinkle feta evenly across dough and gently press into filling to secure. Roll lengthwise to form a log shape.
5. Cut the roll into twelve 1" pieces. Brush with egg. Place in the air fryer basket and cook 15 minutes, turning halfway through cooking time.
6. Let cool 5 minutes before serving.

Cheese And Bean Enchiladas

Servings: 4
Cooking Time: 9 Minutes
Ingredients:
- 1 can pinto beans, drained and rinsed
- 1 ½ tablespoons taco seasoning
- 1 cup red enchilada sauce, divided
- 1 ½ cups shredded Mexican-blend cheese, divided
- 4 fajita-size flour tortillas

Directions:
1. Preheat the air fryer to 320°F (160°C).
2. In a large microwave-safe bowl, microwave beans for 1 minute. Mash half the beans and fold into whole beans. Mix in taco seasoning, ¼ cup enchilada sauce, and 1 cup cheese until well combined.
3. Place ¼ cup bean mixture onto each tortilla. Fold up one end about 1", then roll to close.
4. Place enchiladas into a 3-quart baking pan, pushing together as needed to make them fit. Pour remaining ¾ cup enchilada sauce over enchiladas and top with remaining ½ cup cheese.
5. Place pan in the air fryer basket and cook 8 minutes until cheese is brown and bubbling and the edges of tortillas are brown. Serve warm.

Wine Infused Mushrooms

Servings: 6
Cooking Time: 32 Minutes
Ingredients:
- 1 tablespoon butter
- 2 teaspoons Herbs de Provence
- ½ teaspoon garlic powder
- 2 pounds fresh mushrooms, quartered
- 2 tablespoons white vermouth

Directions:
1. Set the temperature of air fryer to 320°F (160°C).
2. In an air fryer pan, mix together the butter, Herbs de Provence, and garlic powder and air fry for about 2 minutes.
3. Stir in the mushrooms and air fry for about 25 minutes.
4. Stir in the vermouth and air fry for 5 more minutes.
5. Remove from air fryer and transfer the mushrooms onto serving plates.
6. Serve hot.

Twice-baked Broccoli-cheddar Potatoes

Servings: 4
Cooking Time: 35 Minutes
Ingredients:
- 4 large russet potatoes
- 2 tablespoons plus 2 teaspoons ranch dressing
- 1 teaspoon salt
- ½ teaspoon ground black pepper
- ¼ cup chopped cooked broccoli florets
- 1 cup shredded sharp Cheddar cheese

Directions:
1. Preheat the air fryer to 400°F (205°C).
2. Using a fork, poke several holes in potatoes. Place in the air fryer basket and cook 30 minutes until fork-tender.
3. Once potatoes are cool enough to handle, slice lengthwise and scoop out the cooked potato into a large bowl, being careful to maintain the structural integrity of potato skins. Add ranch dressing, salt, pepper, broccoli, and Cheddar to potato flesh and stir until well combined.
4. Scoop potato mixture back into potato skins and return to the air fryer basket. Cook an additional 5 minutes until cheese is melted. Serve warm.

Basil Tomatoes

Servings: 2
Cooking Time: 10 Minutes
Ingredients:
- 2 tomatoes, halved
- 1 tablespoon fresh basil, chopped
- Olive oil cooking spray
- Salt and black pepper, as required

Directions:
1. Preheat the Air fryer to 320°F (160°C) and grease an Air fryer basket.
2. Spray the tomato halves evenly with olive oil cooking spray and season with salt, black pepper and basil.
3. Arrange the tomato halves into the Air fryer basket, cut sides up.
4. Cook for about 10 minutes and dish out onto serving plates.

Lemon Caper Cauliflower Steaks

Servings: 4
Cooking Time: 15 Minutes
Ingredients:
- 1 small head cauliflower, leaves and core removed, cut into 4 (½"-thick) "steaks"
- 4 tablespoons olive oil, divided
- 1 medium lemon, zested and juiced, divided
- ¼ teaspoon salt
- ⅛ teaspoon ground black pepper
- 1 tablespoon salted butter, melted
- 1 tablespoon capers, rinsed

Directions:
1. Brush each cauliflower "steak" with ½ tablespoon olive oil on both sides and sprinkle with lemon zest, salt, and pepper on both sides.
2. Place cauliflower into ungreased air fryer basket. Adjust the temperature to 400°F (205°C) and set the timer for 15 minutes, turning cauliflower halfway through cooking. Steaks will be golden at the edges and browned when done.
3. Transfer steaks to four medium plates. In a small bowl, whisk remaining olive oil, butter, lemon juice, and capers, and pour evenly over steaks. Serve warm.

Crispy Eggplant Rounds

Servings: 4
Cooking Time: 10 Minutes
Ingredients:
- 1 large eggplant, ends trimmed, cut into ½" slices
- ½ teaspoon salt
- 2 ounces Parmesan 100% cheese crisps, finely ground
- ½ teaspoon paprika
- ¼ teaspoon garlic powder
- 1 large egg

Directions:
1. Sprinkle eggplant rounds with salt. Place rounds on a kitchen towel for 30 minutes to draw out excess water. Pat rounds dry.
2. In a medium bowl, mix cheese crisps, paprika, and garlic powder. In a separate medium bowl, whisk egg. Dip each eggplant round in egg, then gently press into cheese crisps to coat both sides.
3. Place eggplant rounds into ungreased air fryer basket. Adjust the temperature to 400°F (205°C) and set the timer for 10 minutes, turning rounds halfway through cooking. Eggplant will be golden and crispy when done. Serve warm.

Curried Eggplant

Servings: 2
Cooking Time: 10 Minutes
Ingredients:
- 1 large eggplant, cut into ½-inch thick slices
- 1 garlic clove, minced
- ½ fresh red chili, chopped
- 1 tablespoon vegetable oil
- ¼ teaspoon curry powder
- Salt, to taste

Directions:
1. Preheat the Air fryer to 300°F (150°C) and grease an Air fryer basket.
2. Mix all the ingredients in a bowl and toss to coat well.
3. Arrange the eggplant slices in the Air fryer basket and cook for about 10 minutes, tossing once in between.
4. Dish out onto serving plates and serve hot.

Chapter 7: Fish And Seafood Recipes

Timeless Garlic-lemon Scallops

Servings: 2
Cooking Time: 15 Minutes
Ingredients:
- 2 tbsp butter, melted
- 1 garlic clove, minced
- 1 tbsp lemon juice
- 1 lb jumbo sea scallops

Directions:
1. Preheat air fryer to 400°F. Whisk butter, garlic, and lemon juice in a bowl. Roll scallops in the mixture to coat all sides. Place scallops in the frying basket and Air Fry for 4 minutes, flipping once. Brush the tops of each scallop with butter mixture and cook for 4 more minutes, flipping once. Serve and enjoy!

Lobster Tails

Servings: 4
Cooking Time: 10 Minutes
Ingredients:
- 4 lobster tails
- 2 tablespoons salted butter, melted
- 1 tablespoon finely minced garlic
- ¼ teaspoon salt
- ¼ teaspoon ground black pepper
- 2 tablespoons lemon juice

Directions:
1. Preheat the air fryer to 400°F (205°C).
2. Carefully cut open lobster tails with kitchen scissors and pull back the shell a little to expose the meat. Drizzle butter over each tail, then sprinkle with garlic, salt, and pepper.
3. Place tails in the air fryer basket and cook 10 minutes until lobster is firm and opaque and internal temperature reaches at least 145°F (60°C).
4. Drizzle lemon juice over lobster meat. Serve warm.

Almond Topped Trout

Servings: 4
Cooking Time: 20 Minutes
Ingredients:
- 4 trout fillets
- 2 tbsp olive oil
- Salt and pepper to taste
- 2 garlic cloves, sliced
- 1 lemon, sliced
- 1 tbsp flaked almonds

Directions:
1. Preheat air fryer to 380°F (195°C). Lightly brush each fillet with olive oil on both sides and season with salt and pepper. Put the fillets in a single layer in the frying basket. Put the sliced garlic over the tops of the trout fillets, then top with lemon slices and cook for 12-15 minutes. Serve topped with flaked almonds and enjoy!

Sesame Tuna Steak

Servings: 2
Cooking Time: 12 Minutes
Ingredients:
- 1 tbsp. coconut oil, melted
- 2 x 6-oz. tuna steaks
- ½ tsp. garlic powder
- 2 tsp. black sesame seeds
- 2 tsp. white sesame seeds

Directions:
1. Apply the coconut oil to the tuna steaks with a brunch, then season with garlic powder.
2. Combine the black and white sesame seeds. Embed them in the tuna steaks, covering the fish all over. Place the tuna into your air fryer.
3. Cook for eight minutes at 400°F (205°C), turning the fish halfway through.
4. The tuna steaks are ready when they have reached a temperature of 145°F (60°C). Serve straightaway.

Crunchy Coconut Shrimp

Servings: 2
Cooking Time: 8 Minutes
Ingredients:
- 8 ounces jumbo shrimp, peeled and deveined
- 2 tablespoons salted butter, melted
- ½ teaspoon Old Bay Seasoning
- ¼ cup unsweetened shredded coconut
- ¼ cup coconut flour

Directions:
1. In a large bowl, toss shrimp in butter and Old Bay Seasoning.
2. In a medium bowl, combine shredded coconut with coconut flour. Coat each piece of shrimp in coconut mixture.
3. Place shrimp into ungreased air fryer basket. Adjust the temperature to 400°F (205°C) and set the timer for 8 minutes, gently turning shrimp halfway through cooking. Shrimp will be pink and C-shaped when done. Serve warm.

Maple Butter Salmon

Servings: 4
Cooking Time: 12 Minutes
Ingredients:
- 2 tablespoons salted butter, melted
- 1 teaspoon low-carb maple syrup
- 1 teaspoon yellow mustard
- 4 boneless, skinless salmon fillets
- ½ teaspoon salt

Directions:
1. In a small bowl, whisk together butter, syrup, and mustard. Brush ½ mixture over each fillet on both sides. Sprinkle fillets with salt on both sides.
2. Place salmon into ungreased air fryer basket. Adjust the temperature to 400°F (205°C) and set the timer for 12 minutes. Halfway through cooking, brush fillets on both sides with remaining syrup mixture. Salmon will easily flake and have an internal temperature of at least 145°F (60°C) when done. Serve warm.

Tilapia Fish Fillets

Servings: 2
Cooking Time: 7 Minutes
Ingredients:
- 2 tilapia fillets
- 1 tsp old bay seasoning
- 1/2 tsp butter
- 1/4 tsp lemon pepper
- Pepper
- Salt

Directions:
1. Spray air fryer basket with cooking spray.
2. Place fish fillets into the air fryer basket and season with lemon pepper, old bay seasoning, pepper, and salt.
3. Spray fish fillets with cooking spray and cook at 400°F (205°C) for 7 minutes.
4. Serve and enjoy.

Southern-style Catfish

Servings:4
Cooking Time: 12 Minutes
Ingredients:
- 4 catfish fillets
- ⅓ cup heavy whipping cream
- 1 tablespoon lemon juice
- 1 cup blanched finely ground almond flour
- 2 teaspoons Old Bay Seasoning
- ½ teaspoon salt
- ¼ teaspoon ground black pepper

Directions:
1. Place catfish fillets into a large bowl with cream and pour in lemon juice. Stir to coat.
2. In a separate large bowl, mix flour and Old Bay Seasoning.
3. Remove each fillet and gently shake off excess cream. Sprinkle with salt and pepper. Press each fillet gently into flour mixture on both sides to coat.
4. Place fillets into ungreased air fryer basket. Adjust the temperature to 400°F (205°C) and set the timer for 12 minutes, turning fillets halfway through cooking. Catfish will be golden brown and have an internal temperature of at least 145°F (60°C) when done. Serve warm.

Snow Crab Legs

Servings:6
Cooking Time: 15 Minutes Per Batch
Ingredients:
- 8 pounds fresh shell-on snow crab legs
- 2 tablespoons olive oil
- 2 teaspoons Old Bay Seasoning
- 4 tablespoons salted butter, melted
- 2 teaspoons lemon juice

Directions:
1. Preheat the air fryer to 400°F (205°C).
2. Drizzle crab legs with oil and sprinkle with Old Bay. Place in the air fryer basket, working in batches as necessary. Cook 15 minutes, turning halfway through cooking time, until crab turns a bright red-orange.
3. In a small bowl, whisk together butter and lemon juice. Serve as a dipping sauce with warm crab legs.

Fish Fillet Sandwich

Servings:4
Cooking Time: 18 Minutes
Ingredients:
- 4 cod fillets
- ½ teaspoon salt
- ¼ teaspoon ground black pepper
- 2 cups unsweetened cornflakes, crushed
- 1 cup Italian bread crumbs
- 2 large eggs
- 4 sandwich buns

Directions:
1. Preheat the air fryer to 375°F (190°C).
2. Sprinkle cod with salt and pepper on both sides.
3. In a large bowl, combine cornflakes and bread crumbs.
4. In a medium bowl, whisk eggs. Press each piece of cod into eggs to coat, shaking off excess, then into cornflake mixture to coat evenly on both sides. Spritz with cooking spray.
5. Place in the air fryer basket and cook 18 minutes, turning halfway through cooking time, until fillets are brown and internal temperature reaches at least 145°F (60°C). Place on buns to serve.

Cajun Flounder Fillets

Servings:2
Cooking Time: 5 Minutes
Ingredients:
- 2 4-ounce skinless flounder fillet(s)
- 2 teaspoons Peanut oil
- 1 teaspoon Purchased or homemade Cajun dried seasoning blend

Directions:
1. Preheat the air fryer to 400°F (205°C).
2. Oil the fillet(s) by drizzling on the peanut oil, then gently rubbing in the oil with your clean, dry fingers. Sprinkle the seasoning blend evenly over both sides of the fillet(s).
3. When the machine is at temperature, set the fillet(s) in the basket. If working with more than one fillet, they should not touch, although they may be quite close together, depending on the basket's size. Air-fry undisturbed for 5 minutes, or until lightly browned and cooked through.
4. Use a nonstick-safe spatula to transfer the fillets to a serving platter or plate(s). Serve at once.

Air Fried Calamari

Servings:3
Cooking Time: 30 Minutes
Ingredients:
- ½ cup cornmeal or cornstarch
- 2 large eggs, beaten
- 2 mashed garlic cloves
- 1 cup breadcrumbs
- lemon juice

Directions:
1. Coat calamari with the cornmeal. The first mixture is prepared by mixing the eggs and garlic. Dip the calamari in the eggs' mixture. Then dip them in the breadcrumbs. Put the rings in the fridge for 2 hours.
2. Then, line them in the air fryer and add oil generously. Fry for 10 to 13 minutes at 390°F (200°C), shaking once halfway through. Serve with garlic mayonnaise and top with lemon juice.

Panko-breaded Cod Fillets
Servings: 2
Cooking Time: 20 Minutes
Ingredients:
- 1 lemon wedge, juiced and zested
- ½ cup panko bread crumbs
- Salt to taste
- 1 tbsp Dijon mustard
- 1 tbsp butter, melted
- 2 cod fillets

Directions:
1. Preheat air fryer to 350ºF. Combine all ingredients, except for the fish, in a bowl. Press mixture evenly across tops of cod fillets. Place fillets in the greased frying basket and Air Fry for 10 minutes until the cod is opaque and flakes easily with a fork. Serve immediately.

Cod Nuggets
Servings: 4
Cooking Time: 12 Minutes
Ingredients:
- 2 boneless, skinless cod fillets
- 1 ½ teaspoons salt, divided
- ¾ teaspoon ground black pepper, divided
- 2 large eggs
- 1 cup plain bread crumbs

Directions:
1. Preheat the air fryer to 350°F (175°C).
2. Cut cod fillets into sixteen even-sized pieces. In a large bowl, add cod nuggets and sprinkle with 1 teaspoon salt and ½ teaspoon pepper.
3. In a small bowl, whisk eggs. In another small bowl, mix bread crumbs with remaining ½ teaspoon salt and ¼ teaspoon pepper.
4. One by one, dip nuggets in the eggs, shaking off excess before rolling in the bread crumb mixture. Repeat to make sixteen nuggets.
5. Place nuggets in the air fryer basket and spritz with cooking spray. Cook 12 minutes, turning halfway through cooking time. Nuggets will be done when golden brown and have an internal temperature of at least 145°F (60°C). Serve warm.

Cajun Lobster Tails
Servings: 4
Cooking Time: 10 Minutes
Ingredients:
- 4 lobster tails
- 2 tablespoons salted butter, melted
- 2 teaspoons lemon juice
- 1 tablespoon Cajun seasoning

Directions:
1. Preheat the air fryer to 400°F (205°C).
2. Carefully cut open lobster tails with kitchen scissors and pull back the shell a little to expose the meat. Drizzle butter and lemon juice over each tail, then sprinkle with Cajun seasoning.
3. Place tails in the air fryer basket and cook 10 minutes until lobster shells are bright red and internal temperature reaches at least 145°F (60°C). Serve warm.

Tilapia Teriyaki
Servings: 3
Cooking Time: 10 Minutes
Ingredients:
- 4 tablespoons teriyaki sauce
- 1 tablespoon pineapple juice
- 1 pound tilapia fillets
- cooking spray
- 6 ounces frozen mixed peppers with onions, thawed and drained
- 2 cups cooked rice

Directions:
1. Mix the teriyaki sauce and pineapple juice together in a small bowl.
2. Split tilapia fillets down the center lengthwise.
3. Brush all sides of fish with the sauce, spray air fryer basket with nonstick cooking spray, and place fish in the basket.
4. Stir the peppers and onions into the remaining sauce and spoon over the fish. Save any leftover sauce for drizzling over the fish when serving.
5. Cook at 360°F (180°C) for 10 minutes, until fish flakes easily with a fork and is done in center.
6. Divide into 3 or 4 servings and serve each with approximately ½ cup cooked rice.

Spicy Fish Taco Bowl
Servings: 4
Cooking Time: 12 Minutes
Ingredients:
- ½ teaspoon salt
- ¼ teaspoon garlic powder
- ¼ teaspoon ground cumin
- 4 cod fillets
- 4 cups finely shredded green cabbage
- ⅓ cup mayonnaise
- ¼ teaspoon ground black pepper
- ¼ cup chopped pickled jalapeños

Directions:
1. Sprinkle salt, garlic powder, and cumin over cod and place into ungreased air fryer basket. Adjust the temperature to 350°F (175°C) and set the timer for 12 minutes, turning fillets halfway through cooking. Cod will flake easily and have an internal temperature of at least 145°F (60°C) when done.
2. In a large bowl, toss cabbage with mayonnaise, pepper, and jalapeños until fully coated. Serve cod warm over cabbage slaw on four medium plates.

Thyme Scallops

Servings: 1
Cooking Time: 12 Minutes
Ingredients:
- 1 lb. scallops
- Salt and pepper
- ½ tbsp. butter
- ½ cup thyme, chopped

Directions:
1. Wash the scallops and dry them completely. Season with pepper and salt, then set aside while you prepare the pan.
2. Grease a foil pan in several spots with the butter and cover the bottom with the thyme. Place the scallops on top.
3. Pre-heat the fryer at 400°F (205°C) and set the rack inside.
4. Place the foil pan on the rack and allow to cook for seven minutes.
5. Take care when removing the pan from the fryer and transfer the scallops to a serving dish. Spoon any remaining butter in the pan over the fish and enjoy.

Lemon Pepper-breaded Tilapia

Servings: 4
Cooking Time: 10 Minutes
Ingredients:
- 1 large egg
- ⅓ cup all-purpose flour
- ¼ cup grated Parmesan cheese
- ½ tablespoon lemon pepper seasoning
- 4 boneless, skinless tilapia fillets

Directions:
1. Preheat the air fryer to 375°F (190°C).
2. In a medium bowl, whisk egg. On a large plate, mix flour, Parmesan, and lemon pepper seasoning.
3. Pat tilapia dry. Dip each fillet into egg, gently shaking off excess. Press into flour mixture, then spritz both sides with cooking spray.
4. Place in the air fryer basket and cook 10 minutes, turning halfway through cooking, until fillets are golden and crispy and internal temperature reaches at least 145°F (60°C). Serve warm.

Lemon Butter-dill Salmon

Servings: 4
Cooking Time: 10 Minutes
Ingredients:
- 4 skin-on salmon fillets
- ¾ teaspoon salt
- ½ teaspoon ground black pepper
- 1 medium lemon, halved
- 2 tablespoons salted butter, melted
- 1 teaspoon dried dill

Directions:
1. Preheat the air fryer to 375°F (190°C).
2. Sprinkle salmon with salt and pepper.
3. Juice half the lemon and slice the other half into ¼"-thick pieces. In a small bowl, combine juice with butter. Brush mixture over salmon.
4. Sprinkle dill evenly over salmon. Place lemon slices on top of salmon.
5. Place salmon in the air fryer basket and cook 10 minutes until salmon flakes easily and internal temperature reaches at least 145°F (60°C). Remove lemon slices before serving.

Flounder Fillets

Servings: 4
Cooking Time: 8 Minutes
Ingredients:
- 1 egg white
- 1 tablespoon water
- 1 cup panko breadcrumbs
- 2 tablespoons extra-light virgin olive oil
- 4 4-ounce flounder fillets
- salt and pepper
- oil for misting or cooking spray

Directions:
1. Preheat air fryer to 390°F (200°C).
2. Beat together egg white and water in shallow dish.
3. In another shallow dish, mix panko crumbs and oil until well combined and crumbly.
4. Season flounder fillets with salt and pepper to taste. Dip each fillet into egg mixture and then roll in panko crumbs, pressing in crumbs so that fish is nicely coated.
5. Spray air fryer basket with nonstick cooking spray and add fillets. Cook at 390°F (200°C) for 3minutes.
6. Spray fish fillets but do not turn. Cook 5 minutes longer or until golden brown and crispy. Using a spatula, carefully remove fish from basket and serve.

Chili-lime Shrimp

Servings: 4
Cooking Time: 10 Minutes
Ingredients:
- 1 pound medium shrimp, peeled and deveined
- ½ cup lime juice
- 2 tablespoons olive oil
- 2 tablespoons sriracha
- 1 teaspoon salt
- ¼ teaspoon ground black pepper

Directions:
1. Preheat the air fryer to 375°F (190°C).
2. In an 6" round cake pan, combine all ingredients.
3. Place pan in the air fryer and cook 10 minutes, stirring halfway through cooking time, until the inside of shrimp are pearly white and opaque and internal temperature reaches at least 145°F (60°C). Serve warm.

Lemon Shrimp And Zucchinis

Servings: 4
Cooking Time: 15 Minutes
Ingredients:
- 1 pound shrimp, peeled and deveined
- A pinch of salt and black pepper

- 2 zucchinis, cut into medium cubes
- 1 tablespoon lemon juice
- 1 tablespoon olive oil
- 1 tablespoon garlic, minced

Directions:
1. In a pan that fits the air fryer, combine all the ingredients, toss, put the pan in the machine and cook at 370°F (185°C) for 15 minutes. Divide between plates and serve right away.

Fish Sticks

Servings: 4
Cooking Time: 20 Minutes
Ingredients:
- 1 lb. tilapia fillets, cut into strips
- 1 large egg, beaten
- 2 tsp. Old Bay seasoning
- 1 tbsp. olive oil
- 1 cup friendly bread crumbs

Directions:
1. Pre-heat the Air Fryer at 400°F (205°C).
2. In a shallow dish, combine together the bread crumbs, Old Bay, and oil. Put the egg in a small bowl.
3. Dredge the fish sticks in the egg. Cover them with bread crumbs and put them in the fryer's basket.
4. Cook the fish for 10 minutes or until they turn golden brown.
5. Serve hot.

Herbed Haddock

Servings:2
Cooking Time:8 Minutes
Ingredients:
- 2 haddock fillets
- 2 tablespoons pine nuts
- 3 tablespoons fresh basil, chopped
- 1 tablespoon Parmesan cheese, grated
- ½ cup extra-virgin olive oil
- Salt and black pepper, to taste

Directions:
1. Preheat the Air fryer to 355°F (180°C) and grease an Air fryer basket.
2. Coat the haddock fillets evenly with olive oil and season with salt and black pepper.
3. Place the haddock fillets in the Air fryer basket and cook for about 8 minutes.
4. Dish out the haddock fillets in serving plates.
5. Meanwhile, put remaining ingredients in a food processor and pulse until smooth.
6. Top this cheese sauce over the haddock fillets and serve hot.

Horseradish-crusted Salmon Fillets

Servings:3
Cooking Time: 8 Minutes
Ingredients:
- ½ cup Fresh bread crumbs
- 4 tablespoons (¼ cup/½ stick) Butter, melted and cooled
- ¼ cup Jarred prepared white horseradish
- Vegetable oil spray
- 4 6-ounce skin-on salmon fillets

Directions:
1. Preheat the air fryer to 400°F (205°C).
2. Mix the bread crumbs, butter, and horseradish in a bowl until well combined.
3. Take the basket out of the machine. Generously spray the skin side of each fillet. Pick them up one by one with a nonstick-safe spatula and set them in the basket skin side down with as much air space between them as possible. Divide the bread-crumb mixture between the fillets, coating the top of each fillet with an even layer. Generously coat the bread-crumb mixture with vegetable oil spray.
4. Return the basket to the machine and air-fry undisturbed for 8 minutes, or until the topping has lightly browned and the fish is firm but not hard.
5. Use a nonstick-safe spatula to transfer the salmon fillets to serving plates. Cool for 5 minutes before serving. Because of the butter in the topping, it will stay very hot for quite a while. Take care, especially if you're serving these fillets to children.

Outrageous Crispy Fried Salmon Skin

Servings:4
Cooking Time: 10 Minutes
Ingredients:
- ½ pound salmon skin, patted dry
- 4 tablespoons coconut oil
- Salt and pepper to taste

Directions:
1. Preheat the air fryer for 5 minutes.
2. In a large bowl, combine everything and mix well.
3. Place in the fryer basket and close.
4. Cook for 10 minutes at 400°F (205°C).
5. Halfway through the cooking time, give a good shake to evenly cook the skin.

Catfish Nuggets

Servings: 4
Cooking Time: 7 Minutes Per Batch
Ingredients:
- 2 medium catfish fillets, cut in chunks
- salt and pepper
- 2 eggs
- 2 tablespoons skim milk
- ½ cup cornstarch
- 1 cup panko breadcrumbs, crushed
- oil for misting or cooking spray

Directions:
1. Season catfish chunks with salt and pepper to your liking.
2. Beat together eggs and milk in a small bowl.
3. Place cornstarch in a second small bowl.
4. Place breadcrumbs in a third small bowl.

5. Dip catfish chunks in cornstarch, dip in egg wash, shake off excess, then roll in breadcrumbs.
6. Spray all sides of catfish chunks with oil or cooking spray.
7. Place chunks in air fryer basket in a single layer, leaving space between for air circulation.
8. Cook at 390°F (200°C) for 4minutes, turn, and cook an additional 3 minutes, until fish flakes easily and outside is crispy brown.
9. Repeat steps 7 and 8 to cook remaining catfish nuggets.

Miso-rubbed Salmon Fillets

Servings:3
Cooking Time: 5 Minutes
Ingredients:
- ¼ cup White (shiro) miso paste (usually made from rice and soy beans)
- 1½ tablespoons Mirin or a substitute
- 2½ teaspoons Unseasoned rice vinegar
- Vegetable oil spray
- 3 6-ounce skin-on salmon fillets

Directions:
1. Preheat the air fryer to 400°F (205°C).
2. Mix the miso, mirin, and vinegar in a small bowl until uniform.
3. Remove the basket from the machine. Generously spray the skin side of each fillet. Pick them up one by one with a nonstick-safe spatula and set them in the basket skin side down with as much air space between them as possible. Coat the top of each fillet with the miso mixture, dividing it evenly between them.
4. Return the basket to the machine. Air-fry undisturbed for 5 minutes, or until lightly browned and firm.
5. Use a nonstick-safe spatula to transfer the fillets to serving plates. Cool for only a minute or so before serving.

Italian Baked Cod

Servings:4
Cooking Time: 12 Minutes
Ingredients:
- 4 cod fillets
- 2 tablespoons salted butter, melted
- 1 teaspoon Italian seasoning
- ¼ teaspoon salt
- ½ cup low-carb marinara sauce

Directions:
1. Place cod into an ungreased 6" round nonstick baking dish. Pour butter over cod and sprinkle with Italian seasoning and salt. Top with marinara.
2. Place dish into air fryer basket. Adjust the temperature to 350°F (175°C) and set the timer for 12 minutes. Fillets will be lightly browned, easily flake, and have an internal temperature of at least 145°F (60°C) when done. Serve warm.

Lemon-roasted Salmon Fillets

Servings:3
Cooking Time: 7 Minutes
Ingredients:
- 3 6-ounce skin-on salmon fillets
- Olive oil spray
- 9 Very thin lemon slices
- ¾ teaspoon Ground black pepper
- ¼ teaspoon Table salt

Directions:
1. Preheat the air fryer to 400°F (205°C).
2. Generously coat the skin of each of the fillets with olive oil spray. Set the fillets skin side down on your work surface. Place three overlapping lemon slices down the length of each salmon fillet. Sprinkle them with the pepper and salt. Coat lightly with olive oil spray.
3. Use a nonstick-safe spatula to transfer the fillets one by one to the basket, leaving as much air space between them as possible. Air-fry undisturbed for 7 minutes, or until cooked through.
4. Use a nonstick-safe spatula to transfer the fillets to serving plates. Cool for only a minute or two before serving.

Beer-battered Cod

Servings:3
Cooking Time: 12 Minutes
Ingredients:
- 1½ cups All-purpose flour
- 3 tablespoons Old Bay seasoning
- 1 Large egg(s)
- ¼ cup Amber beer, pale ale, or IPA
- 3 4-ounce skinless cod fillets
- Vegetable oil spray

Directions:
1. Preheat the air fryer to 400°F (205°C).
2. Set up and fill two shallow soup plates or small pie plates on your counter: one with the flour, whisked with the Old Bay until well combined; and one with the egg(s), whisked with the beer until foamy and uniform.
3. Dip a piece of cod in the flour mixture, turning it to coat on all sides. Gently shake off any excess flour and dip the fish in the egg mixture, turning it to coat. Let any excess egg mixture slip back into the rest, then set the fish back in the flour mixture and coat it again, then back in the egg mixture for a second wash, then back in the flour mixture for a third time. Coat the fish on all sides with vegetable oil spray and set it aside. "Batter" the remaining piece(s) of cod in the same way.
4. Set the coated cod fillets in the basket with as much space between them as possible. They should not touch. Air-fry undisturbed for 12 minutes, or until brown and crisp.
5. Use kitchen tongs to gently transfer the fish to a wire rack. Cool for only a couple of minutes before serving.

Tuna-stuffed Tomatoes

Servings: 2
Cooking Time: 5 Minutes
Ingredients:
- 2 medium beefsteak tomatoes, tops removed, seeded, membranes removed
- 2 pouches tuna packed in water, drained
- 1 medium stalk celery, trimmed and chopped
- 2 tablespoons mayonnaise
- ¼ teaspoon salt
- ¼ teaspoon ground black pepper
- 2 teaspoons coconut oil
- ¼ cup shredded mild Cheddar cheese

Directions:
1. Scoop pulp out of each tomato, leaving ½" shell.
2. In a medium bowl, mix tuna, celery, mayonnaise, salt, and pepper. Drizzle with coconut oil. Spoon ½ mixture into each tomato and top each with 2 tablespoons Cheddar.
3. Place tomatoes into ungreased air fryer basket. Adjust the temperature to 320°F (160°C) and set the timer for 5 minutes. Cheese will be melted when done. Serve warm.

Salmon Patties

Servings: 4
Cooking Time: 12 Minutes
Ingredients:
- 1 pouch cooked salmon
- 6 tablespoons panko bread crumbs
- ½ cup mayonnaise
- 2 teaspoons Old Bay Seasoning

Directions:
1. Preheat the air fryer to 350°F (175°C).
2. In a large bowl, combine all ingredients.
3. Divide mixture into four equal portions. Using your hands, form into patties and spritz with cooking spray.
4. Place in the air fryer basket and cook 12 minutes, turning halfway through cooking time, until brown and firm. Serve warm.

Cajun Salmon

Servings: 2
Cooking Time: 7 Minutes
Ingredients:
- 2 boneless, skinless salmon fillets
- 2 tablespoons salted butter, softened
- ⅛ teaspoon cayenne pepper
- ½ teaspoon garlic powder
- 1 teaspoon paprika
- ¼ teaspoon ground black pepper

Directions:
1. Brush both sides of each fillet with butter. In a small bowl, mix remaining ingredients and rub into fish on both sides.
2. Place fillets into ungreased air fryer basket. Adjust the temperature to 390°F (200°C) and set the timer for 7 minutes. Internal temperature will be 145°F (60°C) when done. Serve warm.

Crunchy And Buttery Cod With Ritz Cracker Crust

Servings: 2
Cooking Time: 10 Minutes
Ingredients:
- 4 tablespoons butter, melted
- 8 to 10 RITZ crackers, crushed into crumbs
- 2 cod fillets
- salt and freshly ground black pepper
- 1 lemon

Directions:
1. Preheat the air fryer to 380°F (195°C).
2. Melt the butter in a small saucepan on the stovetop or in a microwavable dish in the microwave, and then transfer the butter to a shallow dish. Place the crushed RITZ crackers into a second shallow dish.
3. Season the fish fillets with salt and freshly ground black pepper. Dip them into the butter and then coat both sides with the RITZ crackers.
4. Place the fish into the air fryer basket and air-fry at 380°F (195°C) for 10 minutes, flipping the fish over halfway through the cooking time.
5. Serve with a wedge of lemon to squeeze over the top.

Tortilla-crusted With Lemon Filets

Servings: 4
Cooking Time: 15 Minutes
Ingredients:
- 1 cup tortilla chips, pulverized
- 1 egg, beaten
- 1 tablespoon lemon juice
- 4 fillets of white fish fillet
- Salt and pepper to taste

Directions:
1. Preheat the air fryer to 390°F (200°C).
2. Place a grill pan in the air fryer.
3. Season the fish fillet with salt, pepper, and lemon juice.
4. Soak in beaten eggs and dredge in tortilla chips.
5. Place on the grill pan.
6. Cook for 15 minutes.
7. Make sure to flip the fish halfway through the cooking time.

Shrimp Al Pesto

Servings: 4
Cooking Time: 10 Minutes
Ingredients:
- 1 lb peeled shrimp, deveined
- ¼ cup pesto sauce
- 1 lime, sliced
- 2 cups cooked farro

Directions:
1. Preheat air fryer to 360°F (180°C). Coat the shrimp with the pesto sauce in a bowl. Put the shrimp in a single layer in the frying basket. Put the lime slices over the shrimp and Roast for 5 minutes. Remove lime and discard. Serve the shrimp over a bed of farro pilaf. Enjoy!

Ahi Tuna Steaks

Servings: 2
Cooking Time: 14 Minutes
Ingredients:
- 2 ahi tuna steaks
- 2 tablespoons olive oil
- 3 tablespoons everything bagel seasoning

Directions:
1. Preheat the air fryer to 400°F (205°C).
2. Drizzle both sides of steaks with oil. Place seasoning on a medium plate and press each side of tuna steaks into seasoning to form a thick layer.
3. Place steaks in the air fryer basket and cook 14 minutes, turning halfway through cooking time, until internal temperature reaches at least 145°F (60°C) for well-done. Serve warm.

Easy Lobster Tail With Salted Butetr

Servings: 4
Cooking Time: 6 Minutes
Ingredients:
- 2 tablespoons melted butter
- 4 lobster tails
- Salt and pepper to taste

Directions:
1. Preheat the air fryer to 390°F (200°C).
2. Place the grill pan accessory.
3. Cut the lobster through the tail section using a pair of kitchen scissors.
4. Brush the lobster tails with melted butter and season with salt and pepper to taste.
5. Place on the grill pan and cook for 6 minutes.

Crab-stuffed Avocado Boats

Servings: 4
Cooking Time: 7 Minutes
Ingredients:
- 2 medium avocados, halved and pitted
- 8 ounces cooked crabmeat
- ¼ teaspoon Old Bay Seasoning
- 2 tablespoons peeled and diced yellow onion
- 2 tablespoons mayonnaise

Directions:
1. Scoop out avocado flesh in each avocado half, leaving ½" around edges to form a shell. Chop scooped-out avocado.
2. In a medium bowl, combine crabmeat, Old Bay Seasoning, onion, mayonnaise, and chopped avocado. Place ¼ mixture into each avocado shell.
3. Place avocado boats into ungreased air fryer basket. Adjust the temperature to 350°F (175°C) and set the timer for 7 minutes. Avocado will be browned on the top and mixture will be bubbling when done. Serve warm.

Potato-wrapped Salmon Fillets

Servings: 3
Cooking Time: 8 Minutes
Ingredients:
- 1 Large 1-pound elongated yellow potato(es), peeled
- 3 6-ounce, 1½-inch-wide, quite thick skinless salmon fillets
- Olive oil spray
- ¼ teaspoon Table salt
- ¼ teaspoon Ground black pepper

Directions:
1. Preheat the air fryer to 400°F (205°C).
2. Use a vegetable peeler or mandoline to make long strips from the potato(es). You'll need anywhere from 8 to 12 strips per fillet, depending on the shape of the potato and of the salmon fillet.
3. Drape potato strips over a salmon fillet, overlapping the strips to create an even "crust." Tuck the potato strips under the fillet, overlapping the strips underneath to create as smooth a bottom as you can. Wrap the remaining fillet(s) in the same way.
4. Gently turn the fillets over. Generously coat the bottoms with olive oil spray. Turn them back seam side down and generously coat the tops with the oil spray. Sprinkle the salt and pepper over the wrapped fillets.
5. Use a nonstick-safe spatula to gently transfer the fillets seam side down to the basket. It helps to remove the basket from the machine and set it on your work surface (keeping in mind that the basket's hot). Leave as much air space as possible between the fillets. Air-fry undisturbed for 8 minutes, or until golden brown and crisp.
6. Use a nonstick-safe spatula to gently transfer the fillets to serving plates. Cool for a couple of minutes before serving.

Zesty Mahi Mahi

Servings: 3
Cooking Time: 8 Minutes
Ingredients:
- 1½ pounds Mahi Mahi fillets
- 1 lemon, cut into slices
- 1 tablespoon fresh dill, chopped
- ½ teaspoon red chili powder
- Salt and ground black pepper, as required

Directions:
1. Preheat the Air fryer to 375°F (190°C) and grease an Air fryer basket.
2. Season the Mahi Mahi fillets evenly with chili powder, salt, and black pepper.
3. Arrange the Mahi Mahi fillets into the Air fryer basket and top with the lemon slices.
4. Cook for about 8 minutes and dish out
5. Place the lemon slices over the salmon the salmon fillets in the serving plates.
6. Garnish with fresh dill and serve warm.

Simple Salmon Fillets

Servings: 2
Cooking Time: 7 Minutes
Ingredients:
- 2 salmon fillets
- 2 tsp olive oil
- 2 tsp paprika

- Pepper
- Salt

Directions:
1. Rub salmon fillet with oil, paprika, pepper, and salt.
2. Place salmon fillets in the air fryer basket and cook at 390°F (200°C) for 7 minutes.
3. Serve and enjoy.

Sweet Potato-wrapped Shrimp

Servings: 3
Cooking Time: 6 Minutes
Ingredients:
- 24 Long spiralized sweet potato strands
- Olive oil spray
- ¼ teaspoon Garlic powder
- ¼ teaspoon Table salt
- Up to a ⅛ teaspoon Cayenne
- 12 Large shrimp, peeled and deveined

Directions:
1. Preheat the air fryer to 400°F (205°C).
2. Lay the spiralized sweet potato strands on a large swath of paper towels and straighten out the strands to long ropes. Coat them with olive oil spray, then sprinkle them with the garlic powder, salt, and cayenne.
3. Pick up 2 strands and wrap them around the center of a shrimp, with the ends tucked under what now becomes the bottom side of the shrimp. Continue wrapping the remainder of the shrimp.
4. Set the shrimp bottom side down in the basket with as much air space between them as possible. Air-fry undisturbed for 6 minutes, or until the sweet potato strands are crisp and the shrimp are pink and firm.
5. Use kitchen tongs to transfer the shrimp to a wire rack. Cool for only a minute or two before serving.

Garlic And Dill Salmon

Servings: 2
Cooking Time: 8 Minutes
Ingredients:
- 12 ounces salmon filets with skin
- 2 tablespoons melted butter
- 1 tablespoon extra-virgin olive oil
- 2 garlic cloves, minced
- 1 tablespoon fresh dill
- ½ teaspoon sea salt
- ½ lemon

Directions:
1. Pat the salmon dry with paper towels.
2. In a small bowl, mix together the melted butter, olive oil, garlic, and dill.
3. Sprinkle the top of the salmon with sea salt. Brush all sides of the salmon with the garlic and dill butter.
4. Preheat the air fryer to 350°F (175°C).
5. Place the salmon, skin side down, in the air fryer basket. Cook for 6 to 8 minutes, or until the fish flakes in the center.
6. Remove the salmon and plate on a serving platter. Squeeze fresh lemon over the top of the salmon. Serve immediately.

Catalan Sardines With Romesco Sauce

Servings: 2
Cooking Time: 15 Minutes
Ingredients:
- 2 cans skinless, boneless sardines in oil, drained
- ½ cup warmed romesco sauce
- ½ cup bread crumbs

Directions:
1. Preheat air fryer to 350ºF. In a shallow dish, add bread crumbs. Roll in sardines to coat. Place sardines in the greased frying basket and Air Fry for 6 minutes, turning once. Serve with romesco sauce.

Lime Bay Scallops

Servings: 4
Cooking Time: 10 Minutes
Ingredients:
- 2 tbsp butter, melted
- 1 lime, juiced
- ¼ tsp salt
- 1 lb bay scallops
- 2 tbsp chopped cilantro

Directions:
1. Preheat air fryer to 350ºF. Combine all ingredients in a bowl, except for the cilantro. Place scallops in the frying basket and Air Fry for 5 minutes, tossing once. Serve immediately topped with cilantro.

Simple Salmon

Servings: 2
Cooking Time: 10 Minutes
Ingredients:
- 2 salmon fillets
- Salt and black pepper, as required
- 1 tablespoon olive oil

Directions:
1. Preheat the Air fryer to 390°F (200°C) and grease an Air fryer basket.
2. Season each salmon fillet with salt and black pepper and drizzle with olive oil.
3. Arrange salmon fillets into the Air fryer basket and cook for about 10 minutes.
4. Remove from the Air fryer and dish out the salmon fillets onto the serving plates.

Easy-peasy Shrimp

Servings: 2
Cooking Time: 15 Minutes
Ingredients:
- 1 lb tail-on shrimp, deveined
- 2 tbsp butter, melted
- 1 tbsp lemon juice
- 1 tbsp dill, chopped

Directions:
1. Preheat air fryer to 350ºF. Combine shrimp and butter in a bowl. Place shrimp in the greased frying basket and Air Fry for 6 minutes, flipping once. Squeeze lemon juice over and top with dill. Serve hot.

Chapter 8: Poultry Recipes

Pecan-crusted Chicken Tenders

Servings: 4
Cooking Time: 12 Minutes
Ingredients:
- 2 tablespoons mayonnaise
- 1 teaspoon Dijon mustard
- 1 pound boneless, skinless chicken tenders
- ½ teaspoon salt
- ¼ teaspoon ground black pepper
- ½ cup chopped roasted pecans, finely ground

Directions:
1. In a small bowl, whisk mayonnaise and mustard until combined. Brush mixture onto chicken tenders on both sides, then sprinkle tenders with salt and pepper.
2. Place pecans in a medium bowl and press each tender into pecans to coat each side.
3. Place tenders into ungreased air fryer basket in a single layer, working in batches if needed. Adjust the temperature to 375°F (190°C) and set the timer for 12 minutes, turning tenders halfway through cooking. Tenders will be golden brown and have an internal temperature of at least 165°F (60°C) when done. Serve warm.

Garlic Parmesan Drumsticks

Servings: 4
Cooking Time: 25 Minutes
Ingredients:
- 8 chicken drumsticks
- ½ teaspoon salt
- ⅛ teaspoon ground black pepper
- ½ teaspoon garlic powder
- 2 tablespoons salted butter, melted
- ½ cup grated Parmesan cheese
- 1 tablespoon dried parsley

Directions:
1. Sprinkle drumsticks with salt, pepper, and garlic powder. Place drumsticks into ungreased air fryer basket.
2. Adjust the temperature to 400°F (205°C) and set the timer for 25 minutes, turning drumsticks halfway through cooking. Drumsticks will be golden and have an internal temperature of at least 165°F (60°C) when done.
3. Transfer drumsticks to a large serving dish. Pour butter over drumsticks, and sprinkle with Parmesan and parsley. Serve warm.

Crispy "fried" Chicken

Servings: 4
Cooking Time: 14 Minutes
Ingredients:
- ¾ cup all-purpose flour
- ½ teaspoon paprika
- ¼ teaspoon black pepper
- ¼ teaspoon salt
- 2 large eggs
- 1½ cups panko breadcrumbs
- 1 pound boneless, skinless chicken tenders

Directions:
1. Preheat the air fryer to 400°F (205°C).
2. In a shallow bowl, mix the flour with the paprika, pepper, and salt.
3. In a separate bowl, whisk the eggs; set aside.
4. In a third bowl, place the breadcrumbs.
5. Liberally spray the air fryer basket with olive oil spray.
6. Pat the chicken tenders dry with a paper towel. Dredge the tenders one at a time in the flour, then dip them in the egg, and toss them in the breadcrumb coating. Repeat until all tenders are coated.
7. Set each tender in the air fryer, leaving room on each side of the tender to allow for flipping.
8. When the basket is full, cook 4 to 7 minutes, flip, and cook another 4 to 7 minutes.
9. Remove the tenders and let cool 5 minutes before serving. Repeat until all tenders are cooked.

Spinach And Feta Stuffed Chicken Breasts

Servings: 4
Cooking Time: 27 Minutes
Ingredients:
- 1 package frozen spinach, thawed and drained well
- 1 cup feta cheese, crumbled
- ½ teaspoon freshly ground black pepper
- 4 boneless chicken breasts
- salt and freshly ground black pepper
- 1 tablespoon olive oil

Directions:
1. Prepare the filling. Squeeze out as much liquid as possible from the thawed spinach. Rough chop the spinach and transfer it to a mixing bowl with the feta cheese and the freshly ground black pepper.
2. Prepare the chicken breast. Place the chicken breast on a cutting board and press down on the chicken breast with one hand to keep it stabilized. Make an incision about 1-inch long in the fattest side of the breast. Move the knife up and down inside the chicken breast, without poking through either the top or the bottom, or the other side of the breast. The inside pocket should be about 3-inches long, but the opening should only be about 1-inch wide. If this is too difficult, you can make the incision longer, but you will have to be more careful when cooking the chicken breast since this will expose more of the stuffing.
3. Once you have prepared the chicken breasts, use your fingers to stuff the filling into each pocket, spreading the mixture down as far as you can.
4. Preheat the air fryer to 380°F (195°C).
5. Lightly brush or spray the air fryer basket and the chicken breasts with olive oil. Transfer two of the stuffed chicken breasts to the air fryer. Air-fry for 12 minutes, turning the chicken breasts over halfway through the cooking time. Remove the chicken to a resting plate and air-fry the second two breasts for 12 minutes. Return the first batch of chicken to the air fryer with the second

batch and air-fry for 3 more minutes. When the chicken is cooked, an instant read thermometer should register 165°F (60°C) in the thickest part of the chicken, as well as in the stuffing.

6. Remove the chicken breasts and let them rest on a cutting board for 2 to 3 minutes. Slice the chicken on the bias and serve with the slices fanned out.

Hasselback Alfredo Chicken
Servings:4
Cooking Time: 20 Minutes
Ingredients:
- 4 boneless, skinless chicken breasts
- 4 teaspoons coconut oil
- ½ teaspoon salt
- ¼ teaspoon ground black pepper
- 4 strips cooked sugar-free bacon, broken into 24 pieces
- ½ cup Alfredo sauce
- 1 cup shredded mozzarella cheese
- ¼ teaspoon crushed red pepper flakes

Directions:
1. Cut six horizontal slits in the top of each chicken breast. Drizzle with coconut oil and sprinkle with salt and black pepper. Place into an ungreased 6" round nonstick baking dish.
2. Place 1 bacon piece in each slit in chicken breasts. Pour Alfredo sauce over chicken and sprinkle with mozzarella and red pepper flakes.
3. Place dish into air fryer basket. Adjust the temperature to 370°F (185°C) and set the timer for 20 minutes. Chicken will be done when internal temperature is at least 165°F (60°C) and cheese is browned. Serve warm.

Herb-marinated Chicken
Servings: 4
Cooking Time: 25 Minutes
Ingredients:
- 4 chicken breasts
- 2 tsp rosemary, minced
- 2 tsp thyme, minced
- Salt and pepper to taste
- ½ cup chopped cilantro
- 1 lime, juiced
- Cooking spray

Directions:
1. Place chicken in a resealable bag. Add rosemary, thyme, salt, pepper, cilantro, and lime juice. Seal the bag and toss to coat, then place in the refrigerator for 2 hours.
2. Preheat air fryer to 400°F (205°C). Arrange the chicken in a single layer in the greased frying basket. Spray the chicken with cooking oil. Air Fry for 6-7 minutes, then flip the chicken. Cook for another 3 minutes. Serve and enjoy!

Fried Herbed Chicken Wings
Servings: 4
Cooking Time: 11 Minutes
Ingredients:
- 1 tablespoon Emperor herbs chicken spices
- 8 chicken wings
- Cooking spray

Directions:
1. Generously sprinkle the chicken wings with Emperor herbs chicken spices and place in the preheated to 400°F (205°C) air fryer. Cook the chicken wings for 6 minutes from each side.

Basic Chicken Breasts
Servings: 4
Cooking Time: 15 Minutes
Ingredients:
- 2 tsp olive oil
- 4 chicken breasts
- Salt and pepper to taste
- 1 tbsp Italian seasoning

Directions:
1. Preheat air fryer at 350ºF. Rub olive oil over chicken breasts and sprinkle with salt, Italian seasoning and black pepper. Place them in the frying basket and Air Fry for 8-10 minutes. Let rest for 5 minutes before cutting. Store it covered in the fridge for up to 1 week.

Chicken Sausage In Dijon Sauce
Servings: 4
Cooking Time: 20 Minutes
Ingredients:
- 4 chicken sausages
- 1/4 cup mayonnaise
- 2 tablespoons Dijon mustard
- 1 tablespoon balsamic vinegar
- 1/2 teaspoon dried rosemary

Directions:
1. Arrange the sausages on the grill pan and transfer it to the preheated Air Fryer.
2. Grill the sausages at 350°F (175°C) for approximately 13 minutes. Turn them halfway through cooking.
3. Meanwhile, prepare the sauce by mixing the remaining ingredients with a wire whisk. Serve the warm sausages with chilled Dijon sauce. Enjoy!

Garlic Dill Wings
Servings:4
Cooking Time: 25 Minutes
Ingredients:
- 2 pounds bone-in chicken wings, separated at joints
- ½ teaspoon salt
- ½ teaspoon ground black pepper
- ½ teaspoon onion powder
- ½ teaspoon garlic powder
- 1 teaspoon dried dill

Directions:
1. In a large bowl, toss wings with salt, pepper, onion powder, garlic powder, and dill until evenly coated. Place wings into ungreased air fryer basket in a single layer, working in batches if needed.
2. Adjust the temperature to 400°F (205°C) and set the timer for 25 minutes, shaking the basket every 7 minutes

during cooking. Wings should have an internal temperature of at least 165°F (60°C) and be golden brown when done. Serve warm.

Stuffed Chicken
Servings: 2
Cooking Time: 11 Minutes
Ingredients:
- 8 oz chicken fillet
- 3 oz Blue cheese
- ½ teaspoon salt
- ½ teaspoon thyme
- 1 teaspoon sesame oil

Directions:
1. Cut the fillet into halves and beat them gently with the help of the kitchen hammer. After this, make the horizontal cut in every fillet. Sprinkle the chicken with salt and thyme. Then fill it with Blue cheese and secure the cut with the help of the toothpick. Sprinkle the stuffed chicken fillets with sesame oil. Preheat the air fryer to 385°F (195°C). Put the chicken fillets in the air fryer and cook them for 7 minutes. Then carefully flip the chicken fillets on another side and cook for 4 minutes more.

Italian Chicken Thighs
Servings: 4
Cooking Time: 30 Minutes
Ingredients:
- 4 skin-on bone-in chicken thighs
- 2 tbsp. unsalted butter, melted
- 3 tsp. Italian herbs
- ½ tsp. garlic powder
- ¼ tsp. onion powder

Directions:
1. Using a brush, coat the chicken thighs with the melted butter. Combine the herbs with the garlic powder and onion powder, then massage into the chicken thighs. Place the thighs in the fryer.
2. Cook at 380°F (195°C) for 20 minutes, turning the chicken halfway through to cook on the other side.
3. When the thighs have achieved a golden color, test the temperature with a meat thermometer. Once they have reached 165°F (60°C), remove from the fryer and serve.

Lemon Pepper Chicken Wings
Servings: 4
Cooking Time: 16 Minutes
Ingredients:
- 1 lb chicken wings
- 1 tsp lemon pepper
- 1 tbsp olive oil
- 1 tsp salt

Directions:
1. Add chicken wings into the large mixing bowl.
2. Add remaining ingredients over chicken and toss well to coat.
3. Place chicken wings in the air fryer basket.
4. Cook chicken wings for 8 minutes at 400°F (205°C).
5. Turn chicken wings to another side and cook for 8 minutes more.

6. Serve and enjoy.

Paprika Duck
Servings: 6
Cooking Time: 28 Minutes
Ingredients:
- 10 oz duck skin
- 1 teaspoon sunflower oil
- ½ teaspoon salt
- ½ teaspoon ground paprika

Directions:
1. Preheat the air fryer to 375°F (190°C). Then sprinkle the duck skin with sunflower oil, salt, and ground paprika. Put the duck skin in the air fryer and cook it for 18 minutes. Then flip it on another side and cook for 10 minutes more or until it is crunchy from both sides.

Chicken Wrapped In Bacon
Servings: 6
Cooking Time: 25 Minutes
Ingredients:
- 6 rashers unsmoked back bacon
- 1 small chicken breast
- 1 tbsp. garlic soft cheese

Directions:
1. Cut the chicken breast into six bite-sized pieces.
2. Spread the soft cheese across one side of each slice of bacon.
3. Put the chicken on top of the cheese and wrap the bacon around it, holding it in place with a toothpick.
4. Transfer the wrapped chicken pieces to the Air Fryer and cook for 15 minutes at 350°F (175°C).

Chicken Wings
Servings: 4
Cooking Time: 55 Minutes
Ingredients:
- 3 lb. bone-in chicken wings
- ¾ cup flour
- 1 tbsp. old bay seasoning
- 4 tbsp. butter
- Couple fresh lemons

Directions:
1. In a bowl, combine the all-purpose flour and Old Bay seasoning.
2. Toss the chicken wings with the mixture to coat each one well.
3. Pre-heat the Air Fryer to 375°F (190°C).
4. Give the wings a shake to shed any excess flour and place each one in the Air Fryer. You may have to do this in multiple batches, so as to not overlap any.
5. Cook for 30 – 40 minutes, shaking the basket frequently, until the wings are cooked through and crispy.
6. In the meantime, melt the butter in a frying pan over a low heat. Squeeze one or two lemons and add the juice to the pan. Mix well.
7. Serve the wings topped with the sauce.

Celery Chicken Mix
Servings: 4
Cooking Time: 9 Minutes
Ingredients:
- 1 teaspoon fennel seeds
- ½ teaspoon ground celery
- ½ teaspoon salt
- 1 tablespoon olive oil
- 12 oz chicken fillet

Directions:
1. Cut the chicken fillets on 4 chicken chops. In the shallow bowl mix up fennel seeds and olive oil. Rub the chicken chops with salt and ground celery. Preheat the air fryer to 365°F (185°C). Brush the chicken chops with the fennel oil and place it in the air fryer basket. Cook them for 9 minutes.

Chicken Fajita Poppers
Servings:18
Cooking Time: 20 Minutes
Ingredients:
- 1 pound ground chicken thighs
- ½ medium green bell pepper, seeded and finely chopped
- ¼ medium yellow onion, peeled and finely chopped
- ½ cup shredded pepper jack cheese
- 1 packet gluten-free fajita seasoning

Directions:
1. In a large bowl, combine all ingredients. Form mixture into eighteen 2" balls and place in a single layer into ungreased air fryer basket, working in batches if needed.
2. Adjust the temperature to 350°F (175°C) and set the timer for 20 minutes. Carefully use tongs to turn poppers halfway through cooking. When 5 minutes remain on timer, increase temperature to 400°F (205°C) to give the poppers a dark golden-brown color. Shake air fryer basket once more when 2 minutes remain on timer. Serve warm.

Spinach 'n Bacon Egg Cups
Servings:4
Cooking Time: 10 Minutes
Ingredients:
- ¼ cup spinach, chopped finely
- 1 bacon strip, fried and crumbled
- 3 tablespoons butter
- 4 eggs, beaten
- Salt and pepper to taste

Directions:
1. Preheat the air fryer for 5 minutes.
2. In a mixing bowl, combine the eggs, butter, and spinach. Season with salt and pepper to taste.
3. Grease a ramekin with cooking spray and pour the egg mixture inside.
4. Sprinkle with bacon bits.
5. Place the ramekin in the air fryer.
6. Cook for 10 minutes at 350°F (175°C).

Peppery Lemon-chicken Breast
Servings:1
Cooking Time:
Ingredients:
- 1 chicken breast
- 1 teaspoon minced garlic
- 2 lemons, rinds and juice reserved
- Salt and pepper to taste

Directions:
1. Preheat the air fryer.
2. Place all ingredients in a baking dish that will fit in the air fryer.
3. Place in the air fryer basket.
4. Close and cook for 20 minutes at 400°F (205°C).

Bacon Chicken Mix
Servings: 2
Cooking Time: 25 Minutes
Ingredients:
- 2 chicken legs
- 4 oz bacon, sliced
- ½ teaspoon salt
- ½ teaspoon ground black pepper
- 1 teaspoon sesame oil

Directions:
1. Sprinkle the chicken legs with salt and ground black pepper and wrap in the sliced bacon. After this, preheat the air fryer to 385°F (195°C). Put the chicken legs in the air fryer and sprinkle with sesame oil. Cook the bacon chicken legs for 25 minutes.

Chicken Parmesan Casserole
Servings:4
Cooking Time: 20 Minutes
Ingredients:
- 2 cups cubed cooked chicken breast
- ½ teaspoon salt
- ¼ teaspoon ground black pepper
- ¾ cup marinara sauce
- 2 teaspoons Italian seasoning, divided
- 1 cup shredded mozzarella cheese
- ½ cup grated Parmesan cheese

Directions:
1. Preheat the air fryer to 320°F (160°C).
2. In a large bowl, toss chicken with salt, pepper, marinara, and 1 teaspoon Italian seasoning.
3. Scrape mixture into a 6" round baking dish. Top with mozzarella, Parmesan, and remaining 1 teaspoon Italian seasoning.
4. Place in the air fryer basket and cook 20 minutes until the sauce is bubbling and cheese is brown and melted. Serve warm.

Crispy Italian Chicken Thighs
Servings:4
Cooking Time: 25 Minutes
Ingredients:
- ½ cup mayonnaise
- 4 bone-in, skin-on chicken thighs
- 1 teaspoon salt
- ½ teaspoon ground black pepper
- 2 teaspoons Italian seasoning
- 1 cup Italian bread crumbs

Directions:

1. Preheat the air fryer to 370°F (185°C).
2. Brush mayonnaise over chicken thighs on both sides.
3. Sprinkle thighs with salt, pepper, and Italian seasoning.
4. Place bread crumbs into a resealable plastic bag and add thighs. Shake to coat.
5. Remove thighs from bag and spritz with cooking spray. Place in the air fryer basket and cook 25 minutes, turning thighs after 15 minutes, until skin is golden and crispy and internal temperature reaches at least 165°F (75°C).
6. Serve warm.

Chicken Nuggets

Servings: 4
Cooking Time: 10 Minutes
Ingredients:
- 1 pound ground chicken breast
- 1 ½ teaspoons salt, divided
- ¾ teaspoon ground black pepper, divided
- 1 ½ cups plain bread crumbs, divided
- 2 large eggs

Directions:
1. Preheat the air fryer to 400°F (205°C).
2. In a large bowl, mix chicken, 1 teaspoon salt, ½ teaspoon pepper, and ½ cup bread crumbs.
3. In a small bowl, whisk eggs. In a separate medium bowl, mix remaining 1 cup bread crumbs with remaining ½ teaspoon salt and ¼ teaspoon pepper.
4. Scoop 1 tablespoon chicken mixture and flatten it into a nugget shape.
5. Dip into eggs, shaking off excess before rolling in bread crumb mixture. Repeat with remaining chicken mixture to make twenty nuggets.
6. Place nuggets in the air fryer basket and spritz with cooking spray. Cook 10 minutes, turning halfway through cooking time, until internal temperature reaches 165°F (75°C). Serve warm.

Yummy Shredded Chicken

Servings: 2
Cooking Time: 15 Minutes
Ingredients:
- 2 large chicken breasts
- ¼ tsp Pepper
- 1 tsp garlic puree
- 1 tsp mustard
- Salt

Directions:
1. Add all ingredients to the bowl and toss well.
2. Transfer chicken into the air fryer basket and cook at 360°F (180°C) for 15 minutes.
3. Remove chicken from air fryer and shred using a fork.
4. Serve and enjoy.

Salt And Pepper Wings

Servings: 4
Cooking Time: 25 Minutes
Ingredients:
- 2 pounds bone-in chicken wings, separated at joints
- 1 teaspoon salt
- ½ teaspoon ground black pepper

Directions:
1. Sprinkle wings with salt and pepper, then place into ungreased air fryer basket in a single layer, working in batches if needed.
2. Adjust the temperature to 400°F (205°C) and set the timer for 25 minutes, shaking the basket every 7 minutes during cooking. Wings should have an internal temperature of at least 165°F (75°C) and be golden brown when done. Serve warm.

Yummy Stuffed Chicken Breast

Servings: 4
Cooking Time: 15 Minutes
Ingredients:
- 2 chicken fillets, skinless and boneless, each cut into 2 pieces
- 4 brie cheese slices
- 1 tablespoon chive, minced
- 4 cured ham slices
- Salt and black pepper, to taste

Directions:
1. Preheat the Air fryer to 355°F (180°C) and grease an Air fryer basket.
2. Make a slit in each chicken piece horizontally and season with the salt and black pepper.
3. Insert cheese slice in the slits and sprinkle with chives.
4. Wrap each chicken piece with one ham slice and transfer into the Air fryer basket.
5. Cook for about 15 minutes and dish out to serve warm.

Barbecue Chicken Enchiladas

Servings: 4
Cooking Time: 15 Minutes Per Batch
Ingredients:
- 1 ½ cups barbecue sauce, divided
- 3 cups shredded cooked chicken
- 8 flour tortillas
- 1 ½ cups shredded Mexican-blend cheese, divided
- ⅓ cup diced red onion

Directions:
1. Preheat the air fryer to 350°F (175°C).
2. In a large bowl, mix 1 cup barbecue sauce and shredded chicken.
3. Place ¼ cup chicken onto each tortilla and top with 2 tablespoons cheese.
4. Roll each tortilla and place seam side down into two 6" round baking dishes. Brush tortillas with remaining sauce, top with remaining cheese, and sprinkle with onion.
5. Working in batches, place in the air fryer basket and cook 15 minutes until the sauce is bubbling and cheese is melted. Serve warm.

Garlic Ginger Chicken

Servings: 4
Cooking Time: 12 Minutes
Ingredients:
- 1 pound boneless, skinless chicken thighs, cut into 1" pieces
- ¼ cup soy sauce
- 2 cloves garlic, peeled and finely minced

- 1 tablespoon minced ginger
- ¼ teaspoon salt

Directions:
1. Place all ingredients in a large sealable bowl or bag. Place sealed bowl or bag into refrigerator and let marinate at least 30 minutes up to overnight.
2. Remove chicken from marinade and place into ungreased air fryer basket. Adjust the temperature to 375°F (190°C) and set the timer for 12 minutes, shaking the basket twice during cooking. Chicken will be golden and have an internal temperature of at least 165°F (755°C) when done. Serve warm.

Dill Pickle-ranch Wings

Servings:4
Cooking Time: 2 Hours 20 Minutes
Ingredients:
- 1 cup pickle juice
- 2 pounds chicken wings, flats and drums separated
- ½ teaspoon salt
- ½ teaspoon ground black pepper
- 2 teaspoons dry ranch seasoning

Directions:
1. In a large bowl or resealable plastic bag, combine pickle juice and wings. Cover and let marinate in refrigerator 2 hours.
2. Preheat the air fryer to 400°F (205°C).
3. In a separate bowl, mix salt, pepper, and ranch seasoning. Remove wings from marinade and toss in dry seasoning.
4. Place wings in the air fryer basket in a single layer, working in batches as necessary. Cook 20 minutes, turning halfway through cooking time, until wings reach an internal temperature of at least 165°F (75°C). Cool 5 minutes before serving.

Italian Roasted Chicken Thighs

Servings: 6
Cooking Time: 14 Minutes
Ingredients:
- 6 boneless chicken thighs
- ½ teaspoon dried oregano
- ½ teaspoon garlic powder
- ½ teaspoon sea salt
- ½ teaspoon black pepper
- ¼ teaspoon crushed red pepper flakes

Directions:
1. Pat the chicken thighs with paper towel.
2. In a small bowl, mix the oregano, garlic powder, salt, pepper, and crushed red pepper flakes. Rub the spice mixture onto the chicken thighs.
3. Preheat the air fryer to 400°F (205°C).
4. Place the chicken thighs in the air fryer basket and spray with cooking spray. Cook for 10 minutes, turn over, and cook another 4 minutes. When cooking completes, the internal temperature should read 165°F (75°C).

Buffalo Chicken Meatballs

Servings:5
Cooking Time: 12 Minutes
Ingredients:
- 1 pound ground chicken breast
- 1 packet dry ranch seasoning
- ⅓ cup plain bread crumbs
- 3 tablespoons mayonnaise
- 5 tablespoons buffalo sauce, divided

Directions:
1. Preheat the air fryer to 370°F (185°C).
2. In a large bowl, mix chicken, ranch seasoning, bread crumbs, and mayonnaise. Pour in 2 tablespoons buffalo sauce and stir to combine.
3. Roll meat mixture into balls, about 2 tablespoons for each, to make twenty meatballs.
4. Place meatballs in the air fryer basket and cook 12 minutes, shaking the basket twice during cooking, until brown and internal temperature reaches at least 165°F (75°C).
5. Toss meatballs in remaining buffalo sauce and serve.

Blackened Chicken Tenders

Servings:4
Cooking Time: 12 Minutes
Ingredients:
- 1 pound boneless, skinless chicken tenders
- 2 teaspoons paprika
- 1 teaspoon garlic powder
- 1 teaspoon salt
- ½ teaspoon cayenne pepper
- ½ teaspoon dried thyme
- ½ teaspoon ground black pepper
- Cooking spray

Directions:
1. Preheat the air fryer to 400°F (205°C).
2. Place chicken tenders into a large bowl.
3. In a small bowl, mix paprika, garlic powder, salt, cayenne, thyme, and black pepper. Add spice mixture to chicken and toss to coat. Spritz chicken with cooking spray.
4. Place chicken in the air fryer basket and cook 12 minutes, turning halfway through cooking time, until chicken is brown at the edges and internal temperature reaches at least 165°F (75°C). Serve warm.

Quick 'n Easy Garlic Herb Wings

Servings:4
Cooking Time: 35 Minutes
Ingredients:
- ¼ cup chopped rosemary
- 2 pounds chicken wings
- 6 medium garlic cloves, grated
- Salt and pepper to taste

Directions:
1. Season the chicken with garlic, rosemary, salt and pepper.
2. Preheat the air fryer to 390°F (200°C).
3. Place the grill pan accessory in the air fryer.
4. Grill for 35 minutes and make sure to flip the chicken every 10 minutes.

Teriyaki Chicken Kebabs

Servings:4
Cooking Time:1 Hour 15 Minutes
Ingredients:
- ¾ cup teriyaki sauce, divided

- 4 boneless, skinless chicken thighs, cubed
- 1 teaspoon salt
- ½ teaspoon ground black pepper
- 1 cup pineapple chunks
- 1 medium red bell pepper, seeded and cut into 1" cubes
- ¼ medium yellow onion, peeled and cut into 1" cubes

Directions:
1. In a large bowl, pour ½ cup teriyaki sauce over chicken and sprinkle with salt and black pepper. Cover and let marinate in refrigerator 1 hour.
2. Soak eight 6" skewers in water at least 10 minutes to prevent burning. Preheat the air fryer to 400°F (205°C).
3. Place a cube of chicken on skewer, then a piece of pineapple, bell pepper, and onion. Repeat with remaining chicken, pineapple, and vegetables.
4. Brush kebabs with remaining ¼ cup teriyaki sauce and place in the air fryer basket. Cook 15 minutes, turning twice during cooking, until chicken reaches an internal temperature of at least 165°F (75°C) and vegetables are tender. Serve warm.

Easy & Crispy Chicken Wings

Servings: 8
Cooking Time: 20 Minutes
Ingredients:
- 1 1/2 lbs chicken wings
- 2 tbsp olive oil
- Pepper
- Salt

Directions:
1. Toss chicken wings with oil and place in the air fryer basket.
2. Cook chicken wings at 370°F (185°C) for 15 minutes.
3. Shake basket and cook at 400 F for 5 minutes more.
4. Season chicken wings with pepper and salt.
5. Serve and enjoy.

Rosemary Partridge

Servings: 4
Cooking Time: 14 Minutes
Ingredients:
- 10 oz partridges
- 1 teaspoon dried rosemary
- 1 tablespoon butter, melted
- 1 teaspoon salt

Directions:
1. Cut the partridges into the halves and sprinkle with dried rosemary and salt. Then brush them with melted butter. Preheat the air fryer to 385°F (195°C). Put the partridge halves in the air fryer and cook them for 8 minutes. Then flip the poultry on another side and cook for 6 minutes more.

Buttermilk-fried Chicken Thighs

Servings:4
Cooking Time: 1 Hour
Ingredients:
- 1 cup buttermilk
- 2 tablespoons seasoned salt, divided
- 1 pound bone-in, skin-on chicken thighs
- 1 cup all-purpose flour
- ¼ cup cornstarch

Directions:
1. In a large bowl, combine buttermilk and 1 tablespoon seasoned salt. Add chicken. Cover and let marinate in refrigerator 30 minutes.
2. Preheat the air fryer to 375°F (190°C).
3. In a separate bowl, mix flour, cornstarch, and remaining seasoned salt. Dredge chicken thighs, one at a time, in flour mixture, covering completely.
4. Spray chicken generously with cooking spray, being sure that no dry spots remain. Place chicken in the air fryer basket and cook 30 minutes, turning halfway through cooking time and spraying any dry spots, until chicken is dark golden brown and crispy and internal temperature reaches at least 165°F (75°C).
5. Serve warm.

Spice-rubbed Chicken Thighs

Servings:4
Cooking Time: 25 Minutes
Ingredients:
- 4 bone-in, skin-on chicken thighs
- ½ teaspoon salt
- ½ teaspoon garlic powder
- 2 teaspoons chili powder
- 1 teaspoon paprika
- 1 teaspoon ground cumin
- 1 small lime, halved

Directions:
1. Pat chicken thighs dry and sprinkle with salt, garlic powder, chili powder, paprika, and cumin.
2. Squeeze juice from ½ lime over thighs. Place thighs into ungreased air fryer basket. Adjust the temperature to 380°F (195°C) and set the timer for 25 minutes, turning thighs halfway through cooking. Thighs will be crispy and browned with an internal temperature of at least 165°F (75°C) when done.
3. Transfer thighs to a large serving plate and drizzle with remaining lime juice. Serve warm.

Party Buffalo Chicken Drumettes

Servings: 6
Cooking Time: 30 Minutes
Ingredients:
- 16 chicken drumettes
- 1 tsp garlic powder
- 1 tbsp chicken seasoning
- Black pepper to taste
- ¼ cup Buffalo wings sauce
- 2 spring onions, sliced
- Cooking spray

Directions:
1. Preheat air fryer to 400°F (205°C). Sprinkle garlic, chicken seasoning, and black pepper on the drumettes. Place them in the fryer and spray with cooking oil. Air Fry for 10 minutes, shaking the basket once. Transfer the drumettes to a large bowl. Drizzle with Buffalo wing sauce and toss to coat. Place in the fryer and Fry for 7-8 minutes, until crispy. Allow to cool slightly. Top with spring onions and serve warm.

Breaded Chicken Patties

Servings: 4
Cooking Time: 15 Minutes
Ingredients:
- 1 pound ground chicken breast
- 1 cup shredded sharp Cheddar cheese
- ½ cup plain bread crumbs
- 1 teaspoon salt
- ½ teaspoon ground black pepper
- 2 tablespoons mayonnaise
- 1 cup panko bread crumbs
- Cooking spray

Directions:
1. Preheat the air fryer to 400°F (205°C).
2. In a large bowl, mix chicken, Cheddar, plain bread crumbs, salt, and pepper until well combined. Separate into four portions and form into patties ½" thick.
3. Brush each patty with mayonnaise, then press into panko bread crumbs to fully coat. Spritz with cooking spray.
4. Place in the air fryer basket and cook 15 minutes, turning halfway through cooking time, until patties are golden brown and internal temperature reaches at least 165°F (75°C). Serve warm.

15-minute Chicken

Servings: 4
Cooking Time: 15 Minutes
Ingredients:
- 4 boneless, skinless chicken breasts
- 2 tablespoons olive oil
- 1 teaspoon salt
- 1 teaspoon garlic powder
- 1 teaspoon paprika
- ½ teaspoon ground black pepper

Directions:
1. Preheat the air fryer to 375°F (190°C).
2. Carefully butterfly chicken breasts lengthwise, leaving the two halves connected. Drizzle chicken with oil, then sprinkle with salt, garlic powder, paprika, and pepper.
3. Place in the air fryer basket and cook 15 minutes, turning halfway through cooking time, until chicken is golden brown and the internal temperature reaches at least 165°F (75°C). Serve warm.

Zesty Ranch Chicken Drumsticks

Servings: 4
Cooking Time: 20 Minutes
Ingredients:
- 8 chicken drumsticks
- 1 teaspoon salt
- ½ teaspoon ground black pepper
- ¼ cup dry ranch seasoning
- ½ cup panko bread crumbs
- ½ cup grated Parmesan cheese

Directions:
1. Preheat the air fryer to 375°F (190°C).
2. Sprinkle drumsticks with salt, pepper, and ranch seasoning.
3. In a paper lunch bag, combine bread crumbs and Parmesan. Add drumsticks to the bag and shake to coat. Spritz with cooking spray.
4. Place drumsticks in the air fryer basket and cook 20 minutes, turning halfway through cooking time, until the internal temperature reaches at least 165°F (75°C). Serve warm.

Crispy 'n Salted Chicken Meatballs

Servings: 6
Cooking Time: 20 Minutes
Ingredients:
- ½ cup almond flour
- ¾ pound skinless boneless chicken breasts, ground
- 1 ½ teaspoon herbs de Provence
- 1 tablespoon coconut milk
- 2 eggs, beaten
- Salt and pepper to taste

Directions:
1. Mix all ingredient in a bowl.
2. Form small balls using the palms of your hands.
3. Place in the fridge to set for at least 2 hours.
4. Preheat the air fryer for 5 minutes.
5. Place the chicken balls in the fryer basket.
6. Cook for 20 minutes at 325°F (160°C).
7. Halfway through the cooking time, give the fryer basket a shake to cook evenly on all sides.

Sticky Drumsticks

Servings: 4
Cooking Time: 45 Minutes
Ingredients:
- 1 lb chicken drumsticks
- 1 tbsp chicken seasoning
- 1 tsp dried chili flakes
- Salt and pepper to taste
- ¼ cup honey
- 1 cup barbecue sauce

Directions:
1. Preheat air fryer to 390°F (200°C). Season drumsticks with chicken seasoning, chili flakes, salt, and pepper. Place one batch of drumsticks in the greased frying basket and Air Fry for 18-20 minutes, flipping once until golden.
2. While the chicken is cooking, combine honey and barbecue sauce in a small bowl. Remove the drumsticks to a serving dish. Drizzle honey-barbecue sauce over and serve.

Chapter 9: Beef, pork & Lamb Recipes

Peppered Steak Bites

Servings: 4
Cooking Time: 14 Minutes
Ingredients:
- 1 pound sirloin steak, cut into 1-inch cubes
- ½ teaspoon coarse sea salt
- 1 teaspoon coarse black pepper
- 2 teaspoons Worcestershire sauce
- ½ teaspoon garlic powder
- ¼ teaspoon red pepper flakes
- ¼ cup chopped parsley

Directions:
1. Preheat the air fryer to 390°F (200°C).
2. In a large bowl, place the steak cubes and toss with the salt, pepper, Worcestershire sauce, garlic powder, and red pepper flakes.
3. Pour the steak into the air fryer basket and cook for 10 to 14 minutes, depending on how well done you prefer your bites. Starting at the 8-minute mark, toss the steak bites every 2 minutes to check for doneness.
4. When the steak is cooked, remove it from the basket to a serving bowl and top with the chopped parsley. Allow the steak to rest for 5 minutes before serving.

Wasabi-coated Pork Loin Chops

Servings: 3
Cooking Time: 14 Minutes
Ingredients:
- 1½ cups Wasabi peas
- ¼ cup Plain panko bread crumbs
- 1 Large egg white(s)
- 2 tablespoons Water
- 3 5- to 6-ounce boneless center-cut pork loin chops (about ½ inch thick)

Directions:
1. Preheat the air fryer to 375°F (190°C).
2. Put the wasabi peas in a food processor. Cover and process until finely ground, about like panko bread crumbs. Add the bread crumbs and pulse a few times to blend.
3. Set up and fill two shallow soup plates or small pie plates on your counter: one for the egg white(s), whisked with the water until uniform; and one for the wasabi pea mixture.
4. Dip a pork chop in the egg white mixture, coating the chop on both sides as well as around the edge. Allow any excess egg white mixture to slip back into the rest, then set the chop in the wasabi pea mixture. Press gently and turn it several times to coat evenly on both sides and around the edge. Set aside, then dip and coat the remaining chop(s).
5. Set the chops in the basket with as much air space between them as possible. Air-fry, turning once at the 6-minute mark, for 12 minutes, or until the chops are crisp and browned and an instant-read meat thermometer inserted into the center of a chop registers 145°F (60°C). If the machine is at 360°F (180°C), you may need to add 2 minutes to the cooking time.
6. Use kitchen tongs to transfer the chops to a wire rack. Cool for a couple of minutes before serving.

Egg Stuffed Pork Meatballs

Servings: 2
Cooking Time: 40 Minutes
Ingredients:
- 3 soft boiled eggs, peeled
- 8 oz ground pork
- 2 tsp dried tarragon
- ½ tsp hot paprika
- 2 tsp garlic powder
- Salt and pepper to taste

Directions:
1. Preheat air fryer to 350°F (175°C). Combine the pork, tarragon, hot paprika, garlic powder, salt, and pepper in a bowl and stir until all spices are evenly spread throughout the meat. Divide the meat mixture into three equal portions in the mixing bowl, and shape each into balls.
2. Flatten one of the meatballs on top to make a wide, flat meat circle. Place an egg in the middle. Use your hands to mold the mixture up and around to enclose the egg. Repeat with the remaining eggs. Place the stuffed balls in the air fryer. Air Fry for 18-20 minutes, shaking the basket once until the meat is crispy and golden brown. Serve.

Brown Sugar Mustard Pork Loin

Servings: 4
Cooking Time: 35 Minutes
Ingredients:
- 1 pound boneless pork loin
- 1 tablespoon olive oil
- ¼ cup Dijon mustard
- ¼ cup brown sugar
- 1 teaspoon salt
- ½ teaspoon ground black pepper

Directions:
1. Preheat the air fryer to 400°F (205°C). Brush pork loin with oil.
2. In a small bowl, mix mustard, brown sugar, salt, and pepper. Brush mixture over both sides of pork loin and let sit 15 minutes.
3. Place in the air fryer basket and cook 20 minutes until internal temperature reaches 145°F (60°C). Let rest 10 minutes before slicing. Serve warm.

Rib Eye Steak

Servings: 4
Cooking Time: 15 Minutes
Ingredients:
- 4 rib eye steaks
- 1 teaspoon salt
- ½ teaspoon ground black pepper
- 2 tablespoons salted butter

Directions:
1. Preheat the air fryer to 400°F (205°C).
2. Sprinkle steaks with salt and pepper and place in the air fryer basket.

Ninja Air Fryer Cookbook

3. Cook 15 minutes, turning halfway through cooking time, until edges are firm, and the internal temperature reaches at least 160°F (70°C) for well-done.
4. Top each steak with ½ tablespoon butter immediately after removing from the air fryer. Let rest 5 minutes before cutting. Serve warm.

Mexican-style Shredded Beef
Servings: 6
Cooking Time: 35 Minutes
Ingredients:
- 1 beef chuck roast, cut into 2" cubes
- 1 teaspoon salt
- ½ teaspoon ground black pepper
- ½ cup no-sugar-added chipotle sauce

Directions:
1. In a large bowl, sprinkle beef cubes with salt and pepper and toss to coat. Place beef into ungreased air fryer basket. Adjust the temperature to 400°F (205°C) and set the timer for 30 minutes, shaking the basket halfway through cooking. Beef will be done when internal temperature is at least 160°F (70°C).
2. Place cooked beef into a large bowl and shred with two forks. Pour in chipotle sauce and toss to coat.
3. Return beef to air fryer basket for an additional 5 minutes at 400°F (205°C) to crisp with sauce. Serve warm.

Quick & Easy Meatballs
Servings: 4
Cooking Time: 12 Minutes
Ingredients:
- 4 oz lamb meat, minced
- 1 tbsp oregano, chopped
- ½ tbsp lemon zest
- 1 egg, lightly beaten
- Pepper
- Salt

Directions:
1. Add all ingredients into the bowl and mix until well combined.
2. Spray air fryer basket with cooking spray.
3. Make balls from bowl mixture and place into the air fryer basket and cook at 400°F (205°C) for 12 minutes.
4. Serve and enjoy.

Air Fried Thyme Garlic Lamb Chops
Servings: 4
Cooking Time: 12 Minutes
Ingredients:
- 4 lamb chops
- 4 garlic cloves, minced
- 3 tbsp olive oil
- 1 tbsp dried thyme
- Pepper
- Salt

Directions:
1. Preheat the air fryer to 390°F (200°C).
2. Season lamb chops with pepper and salt.
3. In a small bowl, mix together thyme, oil, and garlic and rub over lamb chops.
4. Place lamb chops into the air fryer and cook for 12 minutes. Turn halfway through.
5. Serve and enjoy.

Bacon And Blue Cheese Burgers
Servings: 4
Cooking Time: 15 Minutes
Ingredients:
- 1 pound 70/30 ground beef
- 6 slices cooked sugar-free bacon, finely chopped
- ½ cup crumbled blue cheese
- ¼ cup peeled and chopped yellow onion
- ½ teaspoon salt
- ¼ teaspoon ground black pepper

Directions:
1. In a large bowl, mix ground beef, bacon, blue cheese, and onion. Separate into four sections and shape each section into a patty. Sprinkle with salt and pepper.
2. Place patties into ungreased air fryer basket. Adjust the temperature to 350°F (175°C) and set the timer for 15 minutes, turning patties halfway through cooking. Burgers will be done when internal temperature is at least 150°F (65°C) for medium and 180°F (80°C) for well. Serve warm.

Honey Mesquite Pork Chops
Servings: 2
Cooking Time: 10 Minutes
Ingredients:
- 2 tablespoons mesquite seasoning
- ¼ cup honey
- 1 tablespoon olive oil
- 1 tablespoon water
- freshly ground black pepper
- 2 bone-in center cut pork chops

Directions:
1. Whisk the mesquite seasoning, honey, olive oil, water and freshly ground black pepper together in a shallow glass dish. Pierce the chops all over and on both sides with a fork or meat tenderizer. Add the pork chops to the marinade and massage the marinade into the chops. Cover and marinate for 30 minutes.
2. Preheat the air fryer to 330°F (165°C).
3. Transfer the pork chops to the air fryer basket and pour half of the marinade over the chops, reserving the remaining marinade. Air-fry the pork chops for 6 minutes. Flip the pork chops over and pour the remaining marinade on top. Air-fry for an additional 3 minutes at 330°F (165°C). Then, increase the air fryer temperature to 400°F (205°C) and air-fry the pork chops for an additional minute.
4. Transfer the pork chops to a serving plate, and let them rest for 5 minutes before serving. If you'd like a sauce for these chops, pour the cooked marinade from the bottom of the air fryer over the top.

Parmesan-crusted Pork Chops

Servings: 4
Cooking Time: 12 Minutes
Ingredients:
- 1 large egg
- ½ cup grated Parmesan cheese
- 4 boneless pork chops
- ½ teaspoon salt
- ¼ teaspoon ground black pepper

Directions:
1. Whisk egg in a medium bowl and place Parmesan in a separate medium bowl.
2. Sprinkle pork chops on both sides with salt and pepper. Dip each pork chop into egg, then press both sides into Parmesan.
3. Place pork chops into ungreased air fryer basket. Adjust the temperature to 400°F (205°C) and set the timer for 12 minutes, turning chops halfway through cooking. Pork chops will be golden and have an internal temperature of at least 145°F (60°C) when done. Serve warm.

Sweet And Spicy Spare Ribs

Servings: 6
Cooking Time: 30 Minutes
Ingredients:
- ¼ cup granular brown erythritol
- 2 teaspoons paprika
- 2 teaspoons chili powder
- 1 teaspoon garlic powder
- ½ teaspoon cayenne pepper
- 2 teaspoons salt
- 1 teaspoon ground black pepper
- 1 rack pork spare ribs

Directions:
1. In a small bowl, mix erythritol, paprika, chili powder, garlic powder, cayenne pepper, salt, and black pepper. Rub spice mix over ribs on both sides. Place ribs on ungreased aluminum foil sheet and wrap to cover.
2. Place ribs into ungreased air fryer basket. Adjust the temperature to 400°F (205°C) and set the timer for 25 minutes.
3. When timer beeps, remove ribs from foil, then place back into air fryer basket to cook an additional 5 minutes, turning halfway through cooking. Ribs will be browned and have an internal temperature of at least 180°F (80°C) when done. Serve warm.

Garlic Fillets

Servings: 4
Cooking Time: 15 Minutes
Ingredients:
- 1-pound beef filet mignon
- 1 teaspoon minced garlic
- 1 tablespoon peanut oil
- ½ teaspoon salt
- 1 teaspoon dried oregano

Directions:
1. Chop the beef into the medium size pieces and sprinkle with salt and dried oregano. Then add minced garlic and peanut oil and mix up the meat well. Place the bowl with meat in the fridge for 10 minutes to marinate. Meanwhile, preheat the air fryer to 400°F (205°C). Put the marinated beef pieces in the air fryer and cook them for 10 minutes Then flip the beef on another side and cook for 5 minutes more.

Lemon-butter Veal Cutlets

Servings: 2
Cooking Time: 4 Minutes
Ingredients:
- 3 strips Butter
- 3 Thinly pounded 2-ounce veal leg cutlets (less than ¼ inch thick)
- ¼ teaspoon Lemon-pepper seasoning

Directions:
1. Preheat the air fryer to 400°F (205°C).
2. Run a vegetable peeler lengthwise along a hard, cold stick of butter, making 2, 3, or 4 long strips as the recipe requires for the number of cutlets you're making.
3. Lay the veal cutlets on a clean, dry cutting board or work surface. Sprinkle about ⅛ teaspoon lemon-pepper seasoning over each. Set a strip of butter on top of each cutlet.
4. When the machine is at temperature, set the topped cutlets in the basket so that they don't overlap or even touch. Air-fry undisturbed for 4 minutes without turning.
5. Use a nonstick-safe spatula to transfer the cutlets to a serving plate or plates, taking care to keep as much of the butter on top as possible. Remove the basket from the drawer or from over the baking tray. Carefully pour the browned butter over the cutlets.

Flatiron Steak Grill On Parsley Salad

Servings: 4
Cooking Time: 45 Minutes
Ingredients:
- ½ cup parmesan cheese, grated
- 1 ½ pounds flatiron steak
- 1 tablespoon fresh lemon juice
- 2 cups parsley leaves
- 3 tablespoons olive oil
- Salt and pepper to taste

Directions:
1. Preheat the air fryer to 390°F (200°C).
2. Place the grill pan accessory in the air fryer.
3. Mix together the steak, oil, salt and pepper.
4. Grill for 15 minutes per batch and make sure to flip the meat halfway through the cooking time.
5. Meanwhile, prepare the salad by combining in a bowl the parsley leaves, parmesan cheese and lemon juice. Season with salt and pepper.

Spice-rubbed Pork Loin

Servings: 6
Cooking Time: 20 Minutes
Ingredients:
- 1 teaspoon paprika
- ½ teaspoon ground cumin
- ½ teaspoon chili powder
- ½ teaspoon garlic powder
- 2 tablespoons coconut oil
- 1 boneless pork loin
- ½ teaspoon salt
- ¼ teaspoon ground black pepper

Directions:
1. In a small bowl, mix paprika, cumin, chili powder, and garlic powder.
2. Drizzle coconut oil over pork. Sprinkle pork loin with salt and pepper, then rub spice mixture evenly on all sides.
3. Place pork loin into ungreased air fryer basket. Adjust the temperature to 400°F (205°C) and set the timer for 20 minutes, turning pork halfway through cooking. Pork loin will be browned and have an internal temperature of at least 145°F (60°C) when done. Serve warm.

Mustard Herb Pork Tenderloin

Servings: 6
Cooking Time: 20 Minutes
Ingredients:
- ¼ cup mayonnaise
- 2 tablespoons Dijon mustard
- ½ teaspoon dried thyme
- ¼ teaspoon dried rosemary
- 1 pork tenderloin
- ½ teaspoon salt
- ¼ teaspoon ground black pepper

Directions:
1. In a small bowl, mix mayonnaise, mustard, thyme, and rosemary. Brush tenderloin with mixture on all sides, then sprinkle with salt and pepper on all sides.
2. Place tenderloin into ungreased air fryer basket. Adjust the temperature to 400°F (205°C) and set the timer for 20 minutes, turning tenderloin halfway through cooking. Tenderloin will be golden and have an internal temperature of at least 145°F (60°C) when done. Serve warm.

Mozzarella-stuffed Meatloaf

Servings: 6
Cooking Time: 30 Minutes
Ingredients:
- 1 pound 80/20 ground beef
- ½ medium green bell pepper, seeded and chopped
- ¼ medium yellow onion, peeled and chopped
- ½ teaspoon salt
- ¼ teaspoon ground black pepper
- 2 ounces mozzarella cheese, sliced into ¼"-thick slices
- ¼ cup low-carb ketchup

Directions:
1. In a large bowl, combine ground beef, bell pepper, onion, salt, and black pepper. Cut a piece of parchment to fit air fryer basket. Place half beef mixture on ungreased parchment and form a 9" × 4" loaf, about ½" thick.
2. Center mozzarella slices on beef loaf, leaving at least ¼" around each edge.
3. Press remaining beef into a second 9" × 4" loaf and place on top of mozzarella, pressing edges of loaves together to seal.
4. Place parchment with meatloaf into air fryer basket. Adjust the temperature to 350°F (175°C) and set the timer for 30 minutes, carefully turning loaf and brushing top with ketchup halfway through cooking. Loaf will be browned and have an internal temperature of at least 180°F (80°C) when done. Slice and serve warm.

Pork Belly Marinated In Onion-coconut Cream

Servings: 3
Cooking Time: 25 Minutes
Ingredients:
- ½ pork belly, sliced to thin strips
- 1 onion, diced
- 1 tablespoon butter
- 4 tablespoons coconut cream
- Salt and pepper to taste

Directions:
1. Place all ingredients in a mixing bowl and allow to marinate in the fridge for 2 hours.
2. Preheat the air fryer for 5 minutes.
3. Place the pork strips in the air fryer and bake for 25 minutes at 350°F (175°C).

Easy & The Traditional Beef Roast Recipe

Servings: 12
Cooking Time: 2 Hours
Ingredients:
- 1 cup organic beef broth
- 3 pounds beef round roast
- 4 tablespoons olive oil
- Salt and pepper to taste

Directions:
1. Place in a Ziploc bag all the ingredients and allow to marinate in the fridge for 2 hours.
2. Preheat the air fryer for 5 minutes.
3. Transfer all ingredients in a baking dish that will fit in the air fryer.
4. Place in the air fryer and cook for 2 hours for 400°F (205°C).

Steak Fingers

Servings: 4
Cooking Time: 8 Minutes
Ingredients:
- 4 small beef cube steaks
- salt and pepper

- ½ cup flour
- oil for misting or cooking spray

Directions:
1. Cut cube steaks into 1-inch-wide strips.
2. Sprinkle lightly with salt and pepper to taste.
3. Roll in flour to coat all sides.
4. Spray air fryer basket with cooking spray or oil.
5. Place steak strips in air fryer basket in single layer, very close together but not touching. Spray top of steak strips with oil or cooking spray.
6. Cook at 390°F (200C) for 4minutes, turn strips over, and spray with oil or cooking spray.
7. Cook 4 more minutes and test with fork for doneness. Steak fingers should be crispy outside with no red juices inside. If needed, cook an additional 4 minutes or until well done.
8. Repeat steps 5 through 7 to cook remaining strips.

Barbecue Country-style Pork Ribs

Servings: 3
Cooking Time: 30 Minutes
Ingredients:
- 3 8-ounce boneless country-style pork ribs
- 1½ teaspoons Mild smoked paprika
- 1½ teaspoons Light brown sugar
- ¾ teaspoon Onion powder
- ¾ teaspoon Ground black pepper
- ¼ teaspoon Table salt
- Vegetable oil spray

Directions:
1. Preheat the air fryer to 350°F (175°C) . Set the ribs in a bowl on the counter as the machine heats.
2. Mix the smoked paprika, brown sugar, onion powder, pepper, and salt in a small bowl until well combined. Rub this mixture over all the surfaces of the country-style ribs. Generously coat the country-style ribs with vegetable oil spray.
3. Set the ribs in the basket with as much air space between them as possible. Air-fry undisturbed for 30 minutes, or until browned and sizzling and an instant-read meat thermometer inserted into one rib registers at least 145°F (60°C).
4. Use kitchen tongs to transfer the country-style ribs to a wire rack. Cool for 5 minutes before serving.

Empanadas

Servings:4
Cooking Time: 28 Minutes
Ingredients:
- 1 pound 80/20 ground beef
- ¼ cup taco seasoning
- ⅓ cup salsa
- 2 refrigerated piecrusts
- 1 cup shredded Colby-jack cheese

Directions:
1. In a medium skillet over medium heat, brown beef about 10 minutes until cooked through. Drain fat, then add taco seasoning and salsa to the pan. Bring to a boil, then cook 30 seconds. Reduce heat and simmer 5 minutes. Remove from heat.
2. Preheat the air fryer to 370°F (185°C).
3. Cut three 5" circles from each piecrust, forming six total. Reroll scraps out to ½" thickness. Cut out two more 5" circles to make eight circles total.
4. For each empanada, place ¼ cup meat mixture onto the lower half of a pastry circle and top with 2 tablespoons cheese. Dab a little water along the edge of pastry and fold circle in half to fully cover meat and cheese, pressing the edges together. Use a fork to gently seal the edges. Repeat with remaining pastry, meat, and cheese.
5. Spritz empanadas with cooking spray. Place in the air fryer basket and cook 12 minutes, turning halfway through cooking time, until crust is golden. Serve warm.

Crispy Smoked Pork Chops

Servings: 3
Cooking Time: 8 Minutes
Ingredients:
- ⅔ cup All-purpose flour or tapioca flour
- 1 Large egg white(s)
- 2 tablespoons Water
- 1½ cups Corn flake crumbs (gluten-free, if a concern)
- 3 ½-pound, ½-inch-thick bone-in smoked pork chops

Directions:
1. Preheat the air fryer to 375°F (190°C).
2. Set up and fill three shallow soup plates or small pie plates on your counter: one for the flour; one for the egg white(s), whisked with the water until foamy; and one for the corn flake crumbs.
3. Set a chop in the flour and turn it several times, coating both sides and the edges. Gently shake off any excess flour, then set it in the beaten egg white mixture. Turn to coat both sides as well as the edges. Let any excess egg white slip back into the rest, then set the chop in the corn flake crumbs. Turn it several times, pressing gently to coat the chop evenly on both sides and around the edge. Set the chop aside and continue coating the remaining chop(s) in the same way.
4. Set the chops in the basket with as much air space between them as possible. Air-fry undisturbed for 8 minutes, or until the coating is crunchy and the chops are heated through.
5. Use kitchen tongs to transfer the chops to a wire rack and cool for a couple of minutes before serving.

Sweet And Spicy Pork Ribs

Servings:4
Cooking Time: 20 Minutes Per Batch
Ingredients:
- 1 rack pork spareribs, white membrane removed
- ¼ cup brown sugar
- 2 teaspoons salt
- 2 teaspoons ground black pepper
- 1 tablespoon chili powder
- 1 teaspoon garlic powder

- ½ teaspoon cayenne pepper

Directions:
1. Preheat the air fryer to 400°F (205°C).
2. Place ribs on a work surface and cut the rack into two pieces to fit in the air fryer basket.
3. In a medium bowl, whisk together brown sugar, salt, black pepper, chili powder, garlic powder, and cayenne to make a dry rub.
4. Massage dry rub onto both sides of ribs until well coated. Place a portion of ribs in the air fryer basket, working in batches as necessary.
5. Cook 20 minutes until internal temperature reaches at least 190°F (85°C) and no pink remains. Let rest 5 minutes before cutting and serving.

Cheddar Bacon Ranch Pinwheels

Servings: 5
Cooking Time: 12 Minutes Per Batch
Ingredients:
- 4 ounces full-fat cream cheese, softened
- 1 tablespoon dry ranch seasoning
- ½ cup shredded Cheddar cheese
- 1 sheet frozen puff pastry dough, thawed
- 6 slices bacon, cooked and crumbled

Directions:
1. Preheat the air fryer to 320°F (160°C). Cut parchment paper to fit the air fryer basket.
2. In a medium bowl, mix cream cheese, ranch seasoning, and Cheddar. Unfold puff pastry and gently spread cheese mixture over pastry.
3. Sprinkle crumbled bacon on top. Starting from a long side, roll dough into a log, pressing in the edges to seal.
4. Cut log into ten pieces, then place on parchment in the air fryer basket, working in batches as necessary.
5. Cook 12 minutes, turning each piece after 7 minutes. Let cool 5 minutes before serving.

Bacon And Cheese-stuffed Pork Chops

Servings: 4
Cooking Time: 12 Minutes
Ingredients:
- ½ ounce plain pork rinds, finely crushed
- ½ cup shredded sharp Cheddar cheese
- 4 slices cooked sugar-free bacon, crumbled
- 4 boneless pork chops
- ½ teaspoon salt
- ¼ teaspoon ground black pepper

Directions:
1. In a small bowl, mix pork rinds, Cheddar, and bacon.
2. Make a 3" slit in the side of each pork chop and stuff with ¼ pork rind mixture. Sprinkle each side of pork chops with salt and pepper.
3. Place pork chops into ungreased air fryer basket, stuffed side up. Adjust the temperature to 400°F (205°C) and set the timer for 12 minutes. Pork chops will be browned and have an internal temperature of at least 145°F (60°C) when done. Serve warm.

Venison Backstrap

Servings: 4
Cooking Time: 10 Minutes
Ingredients:
- 2 eggs
- ¼ cup milk
- 1 cup whole wheat flour
- ½ teaspoon salt
- ¼ teaspoon pepper
- 1 pound venison backstrap, sliced
- salt and pepper
- oil for misting or cooking spray

Directions:
1. Beat together eggs and milk in a shallow dish.
2. In another shallow dish, combine the flour, salt, and pepper. Stir to mix well.
3. Sprinkle venison steaks with additional salt and pepper to taste. Dip in flour, egg wash, then in flour again, pressing in coating.
4. Spray steaks with oil or cooking spray on both sides.
5. Cooking in 2 batches, place steaks in the air fryer basket in a single layer. Cook at 360°F (180°C) for 8minutes. Spray with oil, turn over, and spray other side. Cook for 2 minutes longer, until coating is crispy brown and meat is done to your liking.
6. Repeat to cook remaining venison.
7. Spray both sides with oil and cook for 5minutes. If needed, mist with oil and continue cooking for 3 minutes longer. This second batch will cook a little faster than the first because your air fryer is already hot.
8. Serve with marinara sauce on the side for dipping.

Easy-peasy Beef Sliders

Servings: 4
Cooking Time: 25 Minutes
Ingredients:
- 1 lb ground beef
- ¼ tsp cumin
- ¼ tsp mustard power
- 1/3 cup grated yellow onion
- ½ tsp smoked paprika
- Salt and pepper to taste

Directions:
1. Preheat air fryer to 350ºF. Combine the ground beef, cumin, mustard, onion, paprika, salt, and black pepper in a bowl. Form mixture into 8 patties and make a slight indentation in the middle of each. Place beef patties in the greased frying basket and Air Fry for 8-10 minutes, flipping once. Serve right away and enjoy!

Salted 'n Peppered Scored Beef Chuck

Servings: 6
Cooking Time: 1 Hour And 30 Minutes
Ingredients:
- 2 ounces black peppercorns
- 2 tablespoons olive oil
- 3 pounds beef chuck roll, scored with knife

- 3 tablespoons salt

Directions:
1. Preheat the air fryer to 390°F (200°C).
2. Place the grill pan accessory in the air fryer.
3. Season the beef chuck roll with black peppercorns and salt.
4. Brush with olive oil and cover top with foil.
5. Grill for 1 hour and 30 minutes.
6. Flip the beef every 30 minutes for even grilling on all sides.

Orange And Brown Sugar-glazed Ham

Servings:8
Cooking Time: 15 Minutes
Ingredients:
- ½ cup brown sugar
- ¼ cup orange juice
- 2 tablespoons yellow mustard
- 1 fully cooked boneless ham
- 1 teaspoon salt
- ½ teaspoon ground black pepper

Directions:
1. Preheat the air fryer to 375°F (190°C).
2. In a medium bowl, whisk together brown sugar, orange juice, and mustard until combined. Brush over ham until well coated. Sprinkle with salt and pepper.
3. Place in the air fryer basket and cook 15 minutes until heated through and edges are caramelized. Serve warm.

Smokehouse-style Beef Ribs

Servings: 3
Cooking Time: 25 Minutes
Ingredients:
- ¼ teaspoon Mild smoked paprika
- ¼ teaspoon Garlic powder
- ¼ teaspoon Onion powder
- ¼ teaspoon Table salt
- ¼ teaspoon Ground black pepper
- 3 10- to 12-ounce beef back ribs (not beef short ribs)

Directions:
1. Preheat the air fryer to 350°F (175°C).
2. Mix the smoked paprika, garlic powder, onion powder, salt, and pepper in a small bowl until uniform. Massage and pat this mixture onto the ribs.
3. When the machine is at temperature, set the ribs in the basket in one layer, turning them on their sides if necessary, sort of like they're spooning but with at least ¼ inch air space between them. Air-fry for 25 minutes, turning once, until deep brown and sizzling.
4. Use kitchen tongs to transfer the ribs to a wire rack. Cool for 5 minutes before serving.

Fajita Flank Steak Rolls

Servings:4
Cooking Time: 12 Minutes
Ingredients:
- 1 pound flank steak
- 4 slices pepper jack cheese
- 1 medium green bell pepper, seeded and chopped
- ½ medium red bell pepper, seeded and chopped
- ¼ cup finely chopped yellow onion
- 1 teaspoon salt
- ½ teaspoon ground black pepper
- Cooking spray

Directions:
1. Preheat the air fryer to 400°F (205°C).
2. Carefully butterfly steak, leaving the two halves connected. Place slices of cheese on top of steak. Scatter bell peppers and onion over cheese in an even layer.
3. Place steak so that the grain runs horizontally. Tightly roll up steak and secure it with eight evenly spaced toothpicks or eight sections of butcher's twine.
4. Slice steak into four even rolls. Spritz with cooking spray, then sprinkle with salt and black pepper. Place in the air fryer basket and cook 12 minutes until steak is brown on the edges and internal temperature reaches at least 160°F (70°C) for well-done. Serve.

Stuffed Peppers

Servings:4
Cooking Time: 15 Minutes
Ingredients:
- ½ pound cooked Italian sausage, drained
- 1 can diced tomatoes and green chilies, drained
- 2 teaspoons Italian seasoning
- 1 teaspoon salt
- 4 large green bell peppers, trimmed and seeded
- 1 cup shredded Italian-blend cheese
- Cooking spray

Directions:
1. Preheat the air fryer to 320°F (160°C).
2. In a large bowl, mix sausage, tomatoes and chilies, Italian seasoning, and salt.
3. Spoon one-fourth of meat mixture into each pepper. Sprinkle ¼ cup cheese on top of each pepper. Spritz peppers with cooking spray and place in the air fryer basket.
4. Cook 15 minutes until peppers are tender and cheese is melted and bubbling. Serve warm.

Pork Chops

Servings: 2
Cooking Time: 16 Minutes
Ingredients:
- 2 bone-in, centercut pork chops, 1-inch thick
- 2 teaspoons Worcestershire sauce
- salt and pepper
- cooking spray

Directions:
1. Rub the Worcestershire sauce into both sides of pork chops.
2. Season with salt and pepper to taste.
3. Spray air fryer basket with cooking spray and place the chops in basket side by side.
4. Cook at 360°F (180°C) for 16 minutes or until well done. Let rest for 5minutes before serving.

Spinach And Provolone Steak Rolls

Servings: 8
Cooking Time: 12 Minutes
Ingredients:
- 1 flank steak, butterflied
- 8 deli slices provolone cheese
- 1 cup fresh spinach leaves
- ½ teaspoon salt
- ¼ teaspoon ground black pepper

Directions:
1. Place steak on a large plate. Place provolone slices to cover steak, leaving 1" at the edges. Lay spinach leaves over cheese. Gently roll steak and tie with kitchen twine or secure with toothpicks. Carefully slice into eight pieces. Sprinkle each with salt and pepper.
2. Place rolls into ungreased air fryer basket, cut side up. Adjust the temperature to 400°F (200°C) and set the timer for 12 minutes. Steak rolls will be browned and cheese will be melted when done and have an internal temperature of at least 150°F (65°C) for medium steak and 180°F (80°C) for well-done steak. Serve warm.

Rib Eye Steak Seasoned With Italian Herb

Servings: 4
Cooking Time: 45 Minutes
Ingredients:
- 1 packet Italian herb mix
- 1 tablespoon olive oil
- 2 pounds bone-in rib eye steak
- Salt and pepper to taste

Directions:
1. Preheat the air fryer to 390°F (200°C).
2. Place the grill pan accessory in the air fryer.
3. Season the steak with salt, pepper, Italian herb mix, and olive oil. Cover top with foil.
4. Grill for 45 minutes and flip the steak halfway through the cooking time.

Quick & Simple Bratwurst With Vegetables

Servings: 6
Cooking Time: 20 Minutes
Ingredients:
- 1 package bratwurst, sliced 1/2-inch rounds
- 1/2 tbsp Cajun seasoning
- 1/4 cup onion, diced
- 2 bell pepper, sliced

Directions:
1. Add all ingredients into the large mixing bowl and toss well.
2. Line air fryer basket with foil.
3. Add vegetable and bratwurst mixture into the air fryer basket and cook at 390°F (200°C) for 10 minutes.
4. Toss well and cook for 10 minutes more.
5. Serve and enjoy.

Boneless Ribeyes

Servings: 2
Cooking Time: 10-15 Minutes
Ingredients:
- 2 8-ounce boneless ribeye steaks
- 4 teaspoons Worcestershire sauce
- ½ teaspoon garlic powder
- pepper
- 4 teaspoons extra virgin olive oil
- salt

Directions:
1. Season steaks on both sides with Worcestershire sauce. Use the back of a spoon to spread evenly.
2. Sprinkle both sides of steaks with garlic powder and coarsely ground black pepper to taste.
3. Drizzle both sides of steaks with olive oil, again using the back of a spoon to spread evenly over surfaces.
4. Allow steaks to marinate for 30minutes.
5. Place both steaks in air fryer basket and cook at 390°F (200°C) for 5minutes.
6. Turn steaks over and cook until done: medium rare: additional 5 minutes, medium: additional 7 minutes, well done: additional 10 minutes.
7. Remove steaks from air fryer basket and let sit 5minutes. Salt to taste and serve.

Steakhouse Filets Mignons

Servings: 3
Cooking Time: 12-15 Minutes
Ingredients:
- ¾ ounce Dried porcini mushrooms
- ¼ teaspoon Granulated white sugar
- ¼ teaspoon Ground white pepper
- ¼ teaspoon Table salt
- 6 ¼-pound filets mignons or beef tenderloin steaks
- 6 Thin-cut bacon strips (gluten-free, if a concern)

Directions:
1. Preheat the air fryer to 400°F (205°C).
2. Grind the dried mushrooms in a clean spice grinder until powdery. Add the sugar, white pepper, and salt. Grind to blend.
3. Rub this mushroom mixture into both cut sides of each filet. Wrap the circumference of each filet with a strip of bacon.
4. Set the filets mignons in the basket on their sides with the bacon seam side down. Do not let the filets touch; keep at least ¼ inch open between them. Air-fry undisturbed for 12 minutes for rare, or until an instant-read meat thermometer inserted into the center of a filet registers 125°F (50°C); 13 minutes for medium-rare, or until an instant-read meat thermometer inserted into the center of a filet registers 132°F (55°C); or 15 minutes for medium, or until an instant-read meat thermometer inserted into the center of a filet registers 145°F (60°C).
5. Use kitchen tongs to transfer the filets to a wire rack, setting them cut side down. Cool for 5 minutes before serving.

Maple'n Soy Marinated Beef

Servings: 4
Cooking Time: 45 Minutes
Ingredients:
- 2 pounds sirloin flap steaks, pounded
- 3 tablespoons balsamic vinegar
- 3 tablespoons maple syrup
- 3 tablespoons soy sauce
- 4 cloves of garlic, minced

Directions:
1. Preheat the air fryer to 390°F (200°C).
2. Place the grill pan accessory in the air fryer.
3. On a deep dish, place the flap steaks and season with soy sauce, balsamic vinegar, and maple syrup, and garlic.
4. Place on the grill pan and cook for 15 minutes in batches.

Rosemary Lamb Chops

Servings: 4
Cooking Time: 6 Minutes
Ingredients:
- 8 lamb chops
- 1 tablespoon extra-virgin olive oil
- 1 teaspoon dried rosemary, crushed
- 2 cloves garlic, minced
- 1 teaspoon sea salt
- ¼ teaspoon black pepper

Directions:
1. In a large bowl, mix together the lamb chops, olive oil, rosemary, garlic, salt, and pepper. Let sit at room temperature for 10 minutes.
2. Meanwhile, preheat the air fryer to 380°F (195°C).
3. Cook the lamb chops for 3 minutes, flip them over, and cook for another 3 minutes.

Mccornick Pork Chops

Servings: 2
Cooking Time: 15 Minutes
Ingredients:
- 2 pork chops
- 1/2 tsp McCormick Montreal chicken seasoning
- 2 tbsp arrowroot flour
- 1 1/2 tbsp coconut milk
- Salt

Directions:
1. Season pork chops with pepper and salt.
2. Drizzle milk over the pork chops.
3. Place pork chops in a zip-lock bag with flour and shake well to coat. Marinate pork chops for 30 minutes.
4. Place marinated pork chops into the air fryer basket and cook at 380°F (195°C) for 15 minutes. Turn halfway through.
5. Serve and enjoy.

Crispy Ham And Eggs

Servings: 3
Cooking Time: 9 Minutes
Ingredients:
- 2 cups Rice-puff cereal, such as Rice Krispies
- ¼ cup Maple syrup
- ½ pound ¼- to ½-inch-thick ham steak (gluten-free, if a concern)
- 1 tablespoon Unsalted butter
- 3 Large eggs
- ⅛ teaspoon Table salt
- ⅛ teaspoon Ground black pepper

Directions:
1. Preheat the air fryer to 400°F (205°C).
2. Pour the cereal into a food processor, cover, and process until finely ground. Pour the ground cereal into a shallow soup plate or a small pie plate.
3. Smear the maple syrup on both sides of the ham, then set the ham into the ground cereal. Turn a few times, pressing gently, until evenly coated.
4. Set the ham steak in the basket and air-fry undisturbed for 5 minutes, or until browned.
5. Meanwhile, melt the butter in a medium or large nonstick skillet set over medium heat. Crack the eggs into the skillet and cook until the whites are set and the yolks are hot, about 3 minutes. Season with the salt and pepper.
6. When the ham is ready, transfer it to a serving platter, then slip the eggs from the skillet on top of it. Divide into portions to serve.

Air Fried Grilled Steak

Servings: 2
Cooking Time: 45 Minutes
Ingredients:
- 2 top sirloin steaks
- 3 tablespoons butter, melted
- 3 tablespoons olive oil
- Salt and pepper to taste

Directions:
1. Preheat the air fryer for 5 minutes.
2. Season the sirloin steaks with olive oil, salt and pepper.
3. Place the beef in the air fryer basket.
4. Cook for 45 minutes at 350°F (175°C).
5. Once cooked, serve with butter.

Pesto-rubbed Veal Chops

Servings: 2
Cooking Time: 12-15 Minutes
Ingredients:
- ¼ cup Purchased pesto
- 2 10-ounce bone-in veal loin or rib chop(s)
- ½ teaspoon Ground black pepper

Directions:
1. Preheat the air fryer to 400°F (205°C).
2. Rub the pesto onto both sides of the veal chop(s). Sprinkle one side of the chop(s) with the ground black pepper. Set aside at room temperature as the machine comes up to temperature.
3. Set the chop(s) in the basket. If you're cooking more than one chop, leave as much air space between them as possible. Air-fry undisturbed for 12 minutes for medium-

rare, or until an instant-read meat thermometer inserted into the center of a chop registers 135°F (55°C). Or air-fry undisturbed for 15 minutes for medium-well, or until an instant-read meat thermometer registers 145°F (60°C).
4. Use kitchen tongs to transfer the chops to a cutting board or a wire rack. Cool for 5 minutes before serving.

Steak Bites And Spicy Dipping Sauce
Servings:4
Cooking Time: 8 Minutes
Ingredients:
- 2 pounds sirloin steak, cut into 2" cubes
- 2 teaspoons salt
- 1 teaspoon ground black pepper
- 1 teaspoon garlic powder
- ½ cup mayonnaise
- 2 tablespoons sriracha

Directions:
1. Preheat the air fryer to 400°F (205°C).
2. Sprinkle steak with salt, pepper, and garlic powder.
3. Place steak in the air fryer basket and cook 8 minutes, shaking the basket twice during cooking, until internal temperature reaches at least 160°F (70°C).
4. In a small bowl, combine mayonnaise and sriracha. Serve with steak bites for dipping.

Simple Lamb Chops
Servings:2
Cooking Time:6 Minutes
Ingredients:
- 4 lamb chops
- Salt and black pepper, to taste
- 1 tablespoon olive oil

Directions:
1. Preheat the Air fryer to 390°F (200°C) and grease an Air fryer basket.
2. Mix the olive oil, salt, and black pepper in a large bowl and add chops.
3. Arrange the chops in the Air fryer basket and cook for about 6 minutes.
4. Dish out the lamb chops and serve hot.

Lamb Chops
Servings: 2
Cooking Time: 20 Minutes
Ingredients:
- 2 teaspoons oil
- ½ teaspoon ground rosemary
- ½ teaspoon lemon juice
- 1 pound lamb chops, approximately 1-inch thick
- salt and pepper
- cooking spray

Directions:
1. Mix the oil, rosemary, and lemon juice together and rub into all sides of the lamb chops. Season to taste with salt and pepper.
2. For best flavor, cover lamb chops and allow them to rest in the fridge for 20 minutes.
3. Spray air fryer basket with nonstick spray and place lamb chops in it.
4. Cook at 360°F (180°C) for approximately 20 minutes. This will cook chops to medium. The meat will be juicy but have no remaining pink. Cook for a minute or two longer for well done chops. For rare chops, stop cooking after about 12 minutes and check for doneness.

Mustard Pork
Servings: 4
Cooking Time: 30 Minutes
Ingredients:
- 1 pound pork tenderloin, trimmed
- A pinch of salt and black pepper
- 2 tablespoons olive oil
- 3 tablespoons mustard
- 2 tablespoons balsamic vinegar

Directions:
1. In a bowl, mix the pork tenderloin with the rest of the ingredients and rub well. Put the roast in your air fryer's basket and cook at 380°F (195°C) for 30 minutes. Slice the roast, divide between plates and serve.

London Broil
Servings:4
Cooking Time: 12 Minutes
Ingredients:
- 1 pound top round steak
- 1 tablespoon Worcestershire sauce
- ¼ cup soy sauce
- 2 cloves garlic, peeled and finely minced
- ½ teaspoon ground black pepper
- ½ teaspoon salt
- 2 tablespoons salted butter, melted

Directions:
1. Place steak in a large sealable bowl or bag. Pour in Worcestershire sauce and soy sauce, then add garlic, pepper, and salt. Toss to coat. Seal and place into refrigerator to let marinate 2 hours.
2. Remove steak from marinade and pat dry. Drizzle top side with butter, then place into ungreased air fryer basket. Adjust the temperature to 375°F (190°C) and set the timer for 12 minutes, turning steak halfway through cooking. Steak will be done when browned at the edges and it has an internal temperature of 150°F (65°C) for medium or 180°F (80°C) for well-done.
3. Let steak rest on a large plate 10 minutes before slicing into thin pieces. Serve warm.

Greek Pork Chops
Servings: 4
Cooking Time: 30 Minutes
Ingredients:
- 3 tbsp grated Halloumi cheese
- 4 pork chops
- 1 tsp Greek seasoning
- Salt and pepper to taste
- ¼ cup all-purpose flour

- 2 tbsp bread crumbs
- Cooking spray

Directions:
1. Preheat air fryer to 380°F (195°C). Season the pork chops with Greek seasoning, salt and pepper. In a shallow bowl, add flour. In another shallow bowl, combine the crumbs and Halloumi. Dip the chops in the flour, then in the bread crumbs. Place them in the fryer and spray with cooking oil. Bake for 12-14 minutes, flipping once. Serve warm.

Garlic And Oregano Lamb Chops

Servings: 4
Cooking Time: 17 Minutes

Ingredients:
- 1½ tablespoons Olive oil
- 1 tablespoon Minced garlic
- 1 teaspoon Dried oregano
- 1 teaspoon Finely minced orange zest
- ¾ teaspoon Fennel seeds
- ¾ teaspoon Table salt
- ¾ teaspoon Ground black pepper
- 6 4-ounce, 1-inch-thick lamb loin chops

Directions:
1. Mix the olive oil, garlic, oregano, orange zest, fennel seeds, salt, and pepper in a large bowl. Add the chops and toss well to coat. Set aside as the air fryer heats, tossing one more time.
2. Preheat the air fryer to 400°F (205°C).
3. Set the chops bone side down in the basket with as much air space between them as possible. Air-fry undisturbed for 14 minutes for medium-rare, or until an instant-read meat thermometer inserted into the thickest part of a chop registers 132°F (55°C). Or air-fry undisturbed for 17 minutes for well done, or until an instant-read meat thermometer registers 145°F (60°C).
4. Use kitchen tongs to transfer the chops to a wire rack. Cool for 5 minutes before serving.

Roast Beef

Servings: 6
Cooking Time: 60 Minutes

Ingredients:
- 1 top round beef roast
- 1 teaspoon salt
- ½ teaspoon ground black pepper
- 1 teaspoon dried rosemary
- ½ teaspoon garlic powder
- 1 tablespoon coconut oil, melted

Directions:
1. Sprinkle all sides of roast with salt, pepper, rosemary, and garlic powder. Drizzle with coconut oil. Place roast into ungreased air fryer basket, fatty side down. Adjust the temperature to 375°F (190°C) and set the timer for 60 minutes, turning the roast halfway through cooking. Roast will be done when no pink remains and internal temperature is at least 180°F (80°C). Serve warm.

Pork Spare Ribs

Servings: 4
Cooking Time: 30 Minutes

Ingredients:
- 1 rack pork spare ribs
- 1 teaspoon ground cumin
- 2 teaspoons salt
- 1 teaspoon ground black pepper
- 1 teaspoon garlic powder
- ½ teaspoon dry ground mustard
- ½ cup low-carb barbecue sauce

Directions:
1. Place ribs on ungreased aluminum foil sheet. Carefully use a knife to remove membrane and sprinkle meat evenly on both sides with cumin, salt, pepper, garlic powder, and ground mustard.
2. Cut rack into portions that will fit in your air fryer, and wrap each portion in one layer of aluminum foil, working in batches if needed.
3. Place ribs into ungreased air fryer basket. Adjust the temperature to 400°F (205°C) and set the timer for 25 minutes.
4. When the timer beeps, carefully remove ribs from foil and brush with barbecue sauce. Return to air fryer and cook at 400°F (205°C) for an additional 5 minutes to brown. Ribs will be done when no pink remains and internal temperature is at least 180°F (80°C). Serve warm.

Spinach And Mushroom Steak Rolls

Servings: 4
Cooking Time: 19 Minutes

Ingredients:
- ½ medium yellow onion, peeled and chopped
- ½ cup chopped baby bella mushrooms
- 1 cup chopped fresh spinach
- 1 pound flank steak
- 8 slices provolone cheese
- 1 teaspoon salt
- ½ teaspoon ground black pepper
- Cooking spray

Directions:
1. In a medium skillet over medium heat, sauté onion 2 minutes until fragrant and beginning to soften. Add mushrooms and spinach and continue cooking 5 more minutes until spinach is wilted and mushrooms are soft.
2. Preheat the air fryer to 400°F (205°C).
3. Carefully butterfly steak, leaving the two halves connected. Place slices of cheese on top of steak, then top with cooked vegetables.
4. Place steak so that the grain runs horizontally. Tightly roll up steak and secure it closed with eight evenly placed toothpicks or eight sections of butcher's twine.
5. Slice steak into four rolls. Spritz with cooking spray, then sprinkle with salt and pepper. Place in the air fryer basket and cook 12 minutes until steak is brown on the edges and internal temperature reaches at least 160°F (70°C) for well-done. Serve.

Marinated Steak Kebabs

Servings: 4
Cooking Time: 5 Minutes
Ingredients:
- 1 pound strip steak, fat trimmed, cut into 1" cubes
- ½ cup soy sauce
- ¼ cup olive oil
- 1 tablespoon granular brown erythritol
- ½ teaspoon salt
- ¼ teaspoon ground black pepper
- 1 medium green bell pepper, seeded and chopped into 1" cubes

Directions:
1. Place steak into a large sealable bowl or bag and pour in soy sauce and olive oil. Add erythritol, then stir to coat steak. Marinate at room temperature 30 minutes.
2. Remove streak from marinade and sprinkle with salt and black pepper.
3. Place meat and vegetables onto 6" skewer sticks, alternating between steak and bell pepper.
4. Place kebabs into ungreased air fryer basket. Adjust the temperature to 400°F (205°C) and set the timer for 5 minutes. Steak will be done when crispy at the edges and peppers are tender. Serve warm.

Blackened Steak Nuggets

Servings: 2
Cooking Time: 7 Minutes
Ingredients:
- 1 pound rib eye steak, cut into 1" cubes
- 2 tablespoons salted butter, melted
- ½ teaspoon paprika
- ½ teaspoon salt
- ¼ teaspoon garlic powder
- ¼ teaspoon onion powder
- ¼ teaspoon ground black pepper
- ⅛ teaspoon cayenne pepper

Directions:
1. Place steak into a large bowl and pour in butter. Toss to coat. Sprinkle with remaining ingredients.
2. Place bites into ungreased air fryer basket. Adjust the temperature to 400°F (205°C) and set the timer for 7 minutes, shaking the basket three times during cooking. Steak will be crispy on the outside and browned when done and internal temperature is at least 150°F (65°C) for medium and 180°F (80°C) for well-done. Serve warm.

Chicken Fried Steak

Servings: 4
Cooking Time: 15 Minutes
Ingredients:
- 2 eggs
- ½ cup buttermilk
- 1½ cups flour
- ¾ teaspoon salt
- ½ teaspoon pepper
- 1 pound beef cube steaks
- salt and pepper
- oil for misting or cooking spray

Directions:
1. Beat together eggs and buttermilk in a shallow dish.
2. In another shallow dish, stir together the flour, ½ teaspoon salt, and ¼ teaspoon pepper.
3. Season cube steaks with remaining salt and pepper to taste. Dip in flour, buttermilk egg wash, and then flour again.
4. Spray both sides of steaks with oil or cooking spray.
5. Cooking in 2 batches, place steaks in air fryer basket in single layer. Cook at 360°F (1805°C) for 10minutes. Spray tops of steaks with oil and cook 5minutes or until meat is well done.
6. Repeat to cook remaining steaks.

Lamb Burgers

Servings: 2
Cooking Time: 16 Minutes
Ingredients:
- 8 oz lamb, minced
- ½ teaspoon salt
- ½ teaspoon ground black pepper
- ½ teaspoon dried cilantro
- 1 tablespoon water
- Cooking spray

Directions:
1. In the mixing bowl mix up minced lamb, salt, ground black pepper, dried cilantro, and water.
2. Stir the meat mixture carefully with the help of the spoon and make 2 burgers.
3. Preheat the air fryer to 375°F (190°C).
4. Spray the air fryer basket with cooking spray and put the burgers inside.
5. Cook them for 8 minutes from each side.

Chapter 10: Desserts And Sweets

Cocoa Bombs

Servings: 12
Cooking Time: 8 Minutes
Ingredients:
- 2 cups macadamia nuts, chopped
- 4 tablespoons coconut oil, melted
- 1 teaspoon vanilla extract
- ¼ cup cocoa powder
- 1/3 cup swerve

Directions:
1. In a bowl, mix all the ingredients and whisk well. Shape medium balls out of this mix, place them in your air fryer and cook at 300°F (150°C) for 8 minutes. Serve cold.

Cinnamon-sugar Pretzel Bites

Servings: 4
Cooking Time: 1 Hour 10 Minutes
Ingredients:
- 1 cup all-purpose flour
- 1 teaspoon quick-rise yeast
- 2 tablespoons granulated sugar, divided
- ¼ teaspoon salt
- 1 tablespoon olive oil
- 1/3 cup warm water
- 2 teaspoons baking soda
- 1 teaspoon ground cinnamon
- Cooking spray

Directions:
1. In a large bowl, mix flour, yeast, 2 teaspoons sugar, and salt until combined.
2. Pour in oil and water and stir until a dough begins to form and pull away from the edges of the bowl. Remove dough from the bowl and transfer to a lightly floured surface. Knead 10 minutes until dough is mostly smooth.
3. Spritz dough with cooking spray and place into a large clean bowl. Cover with plastic wrap and let rise 1 hour.
4. Preheat the air fryer to 400°F (205°C).
5. Press dough into a 6" × 4" rectangle. Cut dough into twenty-four even pieces.
6. Fill a medium saucepan over medium-high heat halfway with water and bring to a boil. Add baking soda and let it boil 1 minute, then add pretzel bites. You may need to work in batches. Cook 45 seconds, then remove from water and drain. They will be puffy but should have mostly maintained their shape.
7. Spritz pretzel bites with cooking spray. Place in the air fryer basket and cook 5 minutes until golden brown.
8. In a small bowl, mix remaining sugar and cinnamon. When pretzel bites are done cooking, immediately toss in cinnamon and sugar mixture and serve.

Orange Marmalade

Servings: 4
Cooking Time: 20 Minutes
Ingredients:
- 4 oranges, peeled and chopped
- 3 cups sugar
- 1½ cups water

Directions:
1. In a pan that fits your air fryer, mix the oranges with the sugar and the water; stir.
2. Place the pan in the fryer and cook at 340°F (170°C) for 20 minutes.
3. Stir well, divide into cups, refrigerate, and serve cold.

Strawberry Shortcake

Servings: 6
Cooking Time: 25 Minutes
Ingredients:
- 2 tablespoons coconut oil
- 1 cup blanched finely ground almond flour
- 2 large eggs, whisked
- ½ cup granular erythritol
- 1 teaspoon baking powder
- 1 teaspoon vanilla extract
- 2 cups sugar-free whipped cream
- 6 medium fresh strawberries, hulled and sliced

Directions:
1. In a large bowl, combine coconut oil, flour, eggs, erythritol, baking powder, and vanilla. Pour batter into an ungreased 6" round nonstick baking dish.
2. Place dish into air fryer basket. Adjust the temperature to 300°F (150°C) and set the timer for 25 minutes. When done, shortcake should be golden and a toothpick inserted in the middle will come out clean.
3. Remove dish from fryer and let cool 1 hour.
4. Once cooled, top cake with whipped cream and strawberries to serve.

Cinnamon Pretzels

Servings: 6
Cooking Time: 10 Minutes
Ingredients:
- 1½ cups shredded mozzarella cheese
- 1 cup blanched finely ground almond flour
- 2 tablespoons salted butter, melted, divided
- ¼ cup granular erythritol, divided
- 1 teaspoon ground cinnamon

Directions:
1. Place mozzarella, flour, 1 tablespoon butter, and 2 tablespoons erythritol in a large microwave-safe bowl. Microwave on high 45 seconds, then stir with a fork until a smooth dough ball forms.
2. Separate dough into six equal sections. Gently roll each section into a 12" rope, then fold into a pretzel shape.
3. Place pretzels into ungreased air fryer basket. Adjust the temperature to 370°F and set the timer for 8 minutes, turning pretzels halfway through cooking.
4. In a small bowl, combine remaining butter, remaining erythritol, and cinnamon. Brush ½ mixture on both sides of pretzels.
5. Place pretzels back into air fryer and cook an additional 2 minutes at 370°F (185°C).
6. Transfer pretzels to a large plate. Brush on both sides with remaining butter mixture, then let cool 5 minutes before serving.

Crème Brulee

Servings: 3
Cooking Time: 60 Minutes
Ingredients:
- 1 cup milk
- 2 vanilla pods
- 10 egg yolks
- 4 tbsp sugar + extra for topping

Directions:
1. In a pan, add the milk and cream. Cut the vanilla pods open and scrape the seeds into the pan with the vanilla pods also. Place the pan over medium heat on a stovetop until almost boiled while stirring regularly. Turn off the heat. Add the egg yolks to a bowl and beat it. Add the sugar and mix well but not too bubbly.
2. Remove the vanilla pods from the milk mixture; pour the mixture onto the eggs mixture while stirring constantly. Let it sit for 25 minutes. Fill 2 to 3 ramekins with the mixture. Place the ramekins in the fryer basket and cook them at 190°F (85°C) for 50 minutes. Once ready, remove the ramekins and let sit to cool. Sprinkle the remaining sugar over and use a torch to melt the sugar, so it browns at the top.

Apple Pie

Servings: 7
Cooking Time: 25 Minutes
Ingredients:
- 2 large apples
- ½ cup flour
- 2 tbsp. unsalted butter
- 1 tbsp. sugar
- ½ tsp. cinnamon

Directions:
1. Pre-heat the Air Fryer to 360°F (180°C)
2. In a large bowl, combine the flour and butter. Pour in the sugar, continuing to mix.
3. Add in a few tablespoons of water and combine everything to create a smooth dough.
4. Grease the insides of a few small pastry tins with butter. Divide the dough between each tin and lay each portion flat inside.
5. Peel, core and dice up the apples. Put the diced apples on top of the pastry and top with a sprinkling of sugar and cinnamon.
6. Place the pastry tins in your Air Fryer and cook for 15 - 17 minutes.
7. Serve.

Custard

Servings: 4
Cooking Time: 45 Minutes
Ingredients:
- 2 cups whole milk
- 2 eggs
- ¼ cup sugar
- ⅛ teaspoon salt
- ¼ teaspoon vanilla
- cooking spray
- ⅛ teaspoon nutmeg

Directions:
1. In a blender, process milk, egg, sugar, salt, and vanilla until smooth.
2. Spray a 6 x 6-inch baking pan with nonstick spray and pour the custard into it.
3. Cook at 300°F (150°C) for 45 minutes. Custard is done when the center sets.
4. Sprinkle top with the nutmeg.
5. Allow custard to cool slightly.
6. Serve it warm, at room temperature, or chilled.

Fiesta Pastries

Servings: 8
Cooking Time: 20 Minutes
Ingredients:
- ½ of apple, peeled, cored and chopped
- 1 teaspoon fresh orange zest, grated finely
- 7.05-ounce prepared frozen puff pastry, cut into 16 squares
- ½ tablespoon white sugar
- ½ teaspoon ground cinnamon

Directions:
1. Preheat the Air fryer to 390°F (200°C) and grease an Air fryer basket.
2. Mix all ingredients in a bowl except puff pastry.
3. Arrange about 1 teaspoon of this mixture in the center of each square.
4. Fold each square into a triangle and slightly press the edges with a fork.
5. Arrange the pastries in the Air fryer basket and cook for about 10 minutes.
6. Dish out and serve immediately.

Hot Coconut 'n Cocoa Buns

Servings: 8
Cooking Time: 15 Minutes
Ingredients:
- ¼ cup cacao nibs
- 1 cup coconut milk
- 1/3 cup coconut flour
- 3 tablespoons cacao powder
- 4 eggs, beaten

Directions:
1. Preheat the air fryer for 5 minutes.
2. Combine all ingredients in a mixing bowl.
3. Form buns using your hands and place in a baking dish that will fit in the air fryer.
4. Bake for 15 minutes for 375°F (190°C).
5. Once air fryer turns off, leave the buns in the air fryer until it cools completely.

S'mores Pockets

Servings: 6
Cooking Time: 5 Minutes
Ingredients:
- 12 sheets phyllo dough, thawed
- 1½ cups butter, melted

- ¾ cup graham cracker crumbs
- 1 Giant Hershey's milk chocolate bar
- 12 marshmallows, cut in half

Directions:
1. Place one sheet of the phyllo on a large cutting board. Keep the rest of the phyllo sheets covered with a slightly damp, clean kitchen towel. Brush the phyllo sheet generously with some melted butter. Place a second phyllo sheet on top of the first and brush it with more butter. Repeat with one more phyllo sheet until you have a stack of 3 phyllo sheets with butter brushed between the layers. Cover the phyllo sheets with one quarter of the graham cracker crumbs leaving a 1-inch border on one of the short ends of the rectangle. Cut the phyllo sheets lengthwise into 3 strips.
2. Take 2 of the strips and crisscross them to form a cross with the empty borders at the top and to the left. Place 2 of the chocolate rectangles in the center of the cross. Place 4 of the marshmallow halves on top of the chocolate. Now fold the pocket together by folding the bottom phyllo strip up over the chocolate and marshmallows. Then fold the right side over, then the top strip down and finally the left side over. Brush all the edges generously with melted butter to seal shut. Repeat with the next three sheets of phyllo, until all the sheets have been used. You will be able to make 2 pockets with every second batch because you will have an extra graham cracker crumb strip from the previous set of sheets.
3. Preheat the air fryer to 350°F (175°C).
4. Transfer 3 pockets at a time to the air fryer basket. Air-fry at 350°F (175°C) for 4 to 5 minutes, until the phyllo dough is light brown in color. Flip the pockets over halfway through the cooking process. Repeat with the remaining 3 pockets.
5. Serve warm.

Molten Lava Cakes

Servings: 3
Cooking Time: 10 Minutes
Ingredients:
- 2 large eggs
- 1 teaspoon vanilla extract
- ¼ teaspoon salt
- 3 tablespoons unsalted butter
- ¾ cup milk chocolate chips
- ¼ cup all-purpose flour
- Cooking spray

Directions:
1. Preheat the air fryer to 350°F (175°C). Spray three 4" ramekins with cooking spray.
2. In a medium bowl, whisk eggs, vanilla, and salt until well combined.
3. In a large microwave-safe bowl, microwave butter and chocolate chips in 20-second intervals, stirring after each interval, until mixture is fully melted, smooth, and pourable.
4. Whisk chocolate and slowly add egg mixture. Whisk until fully combined.
5. Sprinkle flour into bowl and whisk into chocolate mixture. It should be easily pourable.
6. Divide batter evenly among prepared ramekins. Place in the air fryer basket and cook 5 minutes until the edges and top are set.
7. Let cool 5 minutes and use a butter knife to loosen the edges from ramekins.
8. To serve, place a small dessert plate upside down on top of each ramekin. Quickly flip ramekin and plate upside down so lava cake drops to the plate. Let cool 5 minutes. Serve.

Banana And Rice Pudding

Servings: 6
Cooking Time: 20 Minutes
Ingredients:
- 1 cup brown rice
- 3 cups milk
- 2 bananas, peeled and mashed
- ½ cup maple syrup
- 1 teaspoon vanilla extract

Directions:
1. Place all the ingredients in a pan that fits your air fryer; stir well.
2. Put the pan in the fryer and cook at 360°F (180°C) for 20 minutes.
3. Stir the pudding, divide into cups, refrigerate, and serve cold.

Kiwi Pastry Bites

Servings: 6
Cooking Time: 45 Minutes
Ingredients:
- 3 kiwi fruits, cut into 12 pieces
- 12 wonton wrappers
- ½ cup peanut butter

Directions:
1. Lay out wonton wrappers on a flat, clean surface. Place a kiwi piece on each wrapper, then with 1 tsp of peanut butter. Fold each wrapper from one corner to another to create a triangle. Bring the 2 bottom corners together, but do not seal. Gently press out any air, then press the open edges to seal. Preheat air fryer to 370°F (185°C). Bake the wontons in the greased frying basket for 15-18 minutes, flipping once halfway through cooking, until golden and crisp. Let cool for a few minutes.

Oreo-coated Peanut Butter Cups

Servings: 8
Cooking Time: 4 Minutes
Ingredients:
- 8 Standard ¾-ounce peanut butter cups, frozen
- ⅓ cup All-purpose flour
- 2 Large egg white(s), beaten until foamy
- 16 Oreos or other creme-filled chocolate sandwich cookies, ground to crumbs in a food processor
- Vegetable oil spray

Directions:

1. Set up and fill three shallow soup plates or small pie plates on your counter: one for the flour, one for the beaten egg white(s), and one for the cookie crumbs.
2. Dip a frozen peanut butter cup in the flour, turning it to coat all sides. Shake off any excess, then set it in the beaten egg white(s). Turn it to coat all sides, then let any excess egg white slip back into the rest. Set the candy bar in the cookie crumbs. Turn to coat on all parts, even the sides. Dip the peanut butter cup back in the egg white(s) as before, then into the cookie crumbs as before, making sure you have a solid, even coating all around the cup. Set aside while you dip and coat the remaining cups.
3. When all the peanut butter cups are dipped and coated, lightly coat them on all sides with the vegetable oil spray. Set them on a plate and freeze while the air fryer heats.
4. Preheat the air fryer to 400°F (205°C).
5. Set the dipped cups wider side up in the basket with as much air space between them as possible. Air-fry undisturbed for 4 minutes, or until they feel soft but the coating is set.
6. Turn off the machine and remove the basket from it. Set aside the basket with the fried cups for 10 minutes. Use a nonstick-safe spatula to transfer the fried cups to a wire rack. Cool for at least another 5 minutes before serving.

Marshmallow Pastries

Servings:8
Cooking Time:5 Minutes
Ingredients:
- 4-ounce butter, melted
- 8 phyllo pastry sheets, thawed
- ½ cup chunky peanut butter
- 8 teaspoons marshmallow fluff
- Pinch of salt

Directions:
1. Preheat the Air fryer to 360°F (180°C) and grease an Air fryer basket.
2. Brush butter over 1 filo pastry sheet and top with a second filo sheet.
3. Brush butter over second filo pastry sheet and repeat with all the remaining sheets.
4. Cut the phyllo layers in 8 strips and put 1 tablespoon of peanut butter and 1 teaspoon of marshmallow fluff on the underside of a filo strip.
5. Fold the tip of the sheet over the filling to form a triangle and fold repeatedly in a zigzag manner.
6. Arrange the pastries into the Air fryer basket and cook for about 5 minutes.
7. Season with a pinch of salt and serve warm.

Nutty Fudge Muffins

Servings:10
Cooking Time:10 Minutes
Ingredients:
- 1 package fudge brownie mix
- 1 egg
- 2 teaspoons water
- ¼ cup walnuts, chopped
- 1/3 cup vegetable oil

Directions:
1. Preheat the Air fryer to 300°F (150°C) and grease 10 muffin tins lightly.
2. Mix brownie mix, egg, oil and water in a bowl.
3. Fold in the walnuts and pour the mixture in the muffin cups.
4. Transfer the muffin tins in the Air fryer basket and cook for about 10 minutes.
5. Dish out and serve immediately.

Chocolate Chip Cookie Cake

Servings:8
Cooking Time: 15 Minutes
Ingredients:
- 4 tablespoons salted butter, melted
- ⅓ cup granular brown erythritol
- 1 large egg
- ½ teaspoon vanilla extract
- 1 cup blanched finely ground almond flour
- ½ teaspoon baking powder
- ¼ cup low-carb chocolate chips

Directions:
1. In a large bowl, whisk together butter, erythritol, egg, and vanilla. Add flour and baking powder, and stir until combined.
2. Fold in chocolate chips, then spoon batter into an ungreased 6" round nonstick baking dish.
3. Place dish into air fryer basket. Adjust the temperature to 300°F (150°C) and set the timer for 15 minutes. When edges are browned, cookie cake will be done.
4. Slice and serve warm.

Easy Keto Danish

Servings:6
Cooking Time: 12 Minutes
Ingredients:
- 1½ cups shredded mozzarella cheese
- ½ cup blanched finely ground almond flour
- 3 ounces cream cheese, divided
- ¼ cup confectioners' erythritol
- 1 tablespoon lemon juice

Directions:
1. Place mozzarella, flour, and 1 ounce cream cheese in a large microwave-safe bowl. Microwave on high 45 seconds, then stir with a fork until a soft dough forms.
2. Separate dough into six equal sections and press each in a single layer into an ungreased 4" × 4" square nonstick baking dish to form six even squares that touch.
3. In a small bowl, mix remaining cream cheese, erythritol, and lemon juice. Place 1 tablespoon mixture in center of each piece of dough in baking dish. Fold all four corners of each dough piece halfway to center to reach cream cheese mixture.
4. Place dish into air fryer. Adjust the temperature to 320°F (160°C) and set the timer for 12 minutes. The center and edges will be browned when done. Let cool 10 minutes before serving.

Glazed Donuts

Servings: 2 – 4
Cooking Time: 25 Minutes
Ingredients:
- 1 can [8 oz.] refrigerated croissant dough
- Cooking spray
- 1 can [16 oz.] vanilla frosting

Directions:
1. Cut the croissant dough into 1-inch-round slices. Make a hole in the center of each one to create a donut.
2. Put the donuts in the Air Fryer basket, taking care not to overlap any, and spritz with cooking spray. You may need to cook everything in multiple batches.
3. Cook at 400°F (205°C) for 2 minutes. Turn the donuts over and cook for another 3 minutes.
4. Place the rolls on a paper plate.
5. Microwave a half-cup of frosting for 30 seconds and pour a drizzling of the frosting over the donuts before serving.

Tortilla Fried Pies

Servings: 12
Cooking Time: 5 Minutes
Ingredients:
- 12 small flour tortillas
- ½ cup fig preserves
- ¼ cup sliced almonds
- 2 tablespoons shredded, unsweetened coconut
- oil for misting or cooking spray

Directions:
1. Wrap refrigerated tortillas in damp paper towels and heat in microwave 30 seconds to warm.
2. Working with one tortilla at a time, place 2 teaspoons fig preserves, 1 teaspoon sliced almonds, and ½ teaspoon coconut in the center of each.
3. Moisten outer edges of tortilla all around.
4. Fold one side of tortilla over filling to make a half-moon shape and press down lightly on center. Using the tines of a fork, press down firmly on edges of tortilla to seal in filling.
5. Mist both sides with oil or cooking spray.
6. Place hand pies in air fryer basket close but not overlapping. It's fine to lean some against the sides and corners of the basket. You may need to cook in 2 batches.
7. Cook at 390°F (200°C) for 5 minutes or until lightly browned. Serve hot.
8. Refrigerate any leftover pies in a closed container. To serve later, toss them back in the air fryer basket and cook for 2 or 3 minutes to reheat.

Banana Chips With Chocolate Glaze

Servings: 2
Cooking Time: 20 Minutes
Ingredients:
- 2 banana, cut into slices
- 1/4 teaspoon lemon zest
- 1 tablespoon agave syrup
- 1 tablespoon cocoa powder
- 1 tablespoon coconut oil, melted

Directions:
1. Toss the bananas with the lemon zest and agave syrup. Transfer your bananas to the parchment-lined cooking basket.
2. Bake in the preheated Air Fryer at 370°F (185°C) for 12 minutes, turning them over halfway through the cooking time.
3. In the meantime, melt the coconut oil in your microwave; add the cocoa powder and whisk to combine well.
4. Serve the baked banana chips. Enjoy!

Baked Apple

Servings: 6
Cooking Time: 20 Minutes
Ingredients:
- 3 small Honey Crisp or other baking apples
- 3 tablespoons maple syrup
- 3 tablespoons chopped pecans
- 1 tablespoon firm butter, cut into 6 pieces

Directions:
1. Put ½ cup water in the drawer of the air fryer.
2. Wash apples well and dry them.
3. Split apples in half. Remove core and a little of the flesh to make a cavity for the pecans.
4. Place apple halves in air fryer basket, cut side up.
5. Spoon 1½ teaspoons pecans into each cavity.
6. Spoon ½ tablespoon maple syrup over pecans in each apple.
7. Top each apple with ½ teaspoon butter.
8. Cook at 360°F (180°C) for 20 minutes, until apples are tender.

Hearty Banana Pastry

Servings:2
Cooking Time: 15 Minutes
Ingredients:
- 3 tbsp honey
- 2 puff pastry sheets, cut into thin strips
- fresh berries to serve

Directions:
1. Preheat your air fryer up to 340°F (170C).
2. Place the banana slices into the cooking basket. Cover with the pastry strips and top with honey. Cook for 10 minutes. Serve with fresh berries.

Brown Sugar Cookies

Servings:9
Cooking Time: 27 Minutes
Ingredients:
- 4 tablespoons salted butter, melted
- ⅓ cup granular brown erythritol
- 1 large egg
- ½ teaspoon vanilla extract
- 1 cup blanched finely ground almond flour
- ½ teaspoon baking powder

Directions:

1. In a large bowl, whisk together butter, erythritol, egg, and vanilla. Add flour and baking powder, and stir until combined.
2. Separate dough into nine pieces and roll into balls, about 2 tablespoons each.
3. Cut three pieces of parchment paper to fit your air fryer basket and place three cookies on each ungreased piece. Place one piece of parchment into air fryer basket. Adjust the temperature to 300°F (150°C) and set the timer for 9 minutes. Edges of cookies will be browned when done. Repeat with remaining cookies. Serve warm.

Cinnamon Canned Biscuit Donuts

Servings: 4
Cooking Time: 25 Minutes
Ingredients:
- 1 can jumbo biscuits
- 1 cup cinnamon sugar

Directions:
1. Preheat air fryer to 360°F (180°C). Divide biscuit dough into 8 biscuits and place on a flat work surface. Cut a small circle in the center of the biscuit with a small cookie cutter. Place a batch of 4 donuts in the air fryer. Spray with oil and Bake for 8 minutes, flipping once. Drizzle the cinnamon sugar over the donuts and serve.

Fried Banana S'mores

Servings: 4
Cooking Time: 6 Minutes
Ingredients:
- 4 bananas
- 3 tablespoons mini semi-sweet chocolate chips
- 3 tablespoons mini peanut butter chips
- 3 tablespoons mini marshmallows
- 3 tablespoons graham cracker cereal

Directions:
1. Preheat the air fryer to 400°F (205°C).
2. Slice into the un-peeled bananas lengthwise along the inside of the curve, but do not slice through the bottom of the peel. Open the banana slightly to form a pocket.
3. Fill each pocket with chocolate chips, peanut butter chips and marshmallows. Poke the graham cracker cereal into the filling.
4. Place the bananas in the air fryer basket, resting them on the side of the basket and each other to keep them upright with the filling facing up. Air-fry for 6 minutes, or until the bananas are soft to the touch, the peels have blackened and the chocolate and marshmallows have melted and toasted.
5. Let them cool for a couple of minutes and then simply serve with a spoon to scoop out the filling.

Fried Pineapple Chunks

Servings: 3
Cooking Time: 10 Minutes
Ingredients:
- 3 tablespoons Cornstarch
- 1 Large egg white, beaten until foamy
- 1 cup Ground vanilla wafer cookies (not low-fat cookies)
- ¼ teaspoon Ground dried ginger
- 18 Fresh 1-inch chunks peeled and cored pineapple

Directions:
1. Preheat the air fryer to 400°F (205°C).
2. Put the cornstarch in a medium or large bowl. Put the beaten egg white in a small bowl. Pour the cookie crumbs and ground dried ginger into a large zip-closed plastic bag, shaking it a bit to combine them.
3. Dump the pineapple chunks into the bowl with the cornstarch. Toss and stir until well coated. Use your cleaned fingers or a large fork like a shovel to pick up a few pineapple chunks, shake off any excess cornstarch, and put them in the bowl with the egg white. Stir gently, then pick them up and let any excess egg white slip back into the rest. Put them in the bag with the crumb mixture. Repeat the cornstarch-then-egg process until all the pineapple chunks are in the bag. Seal the bag and shake gently, turning the bag this way and that, to coat the pieces well.
4. Set the coated pineapple chunks in the basket with as much air space between them as possible. Even a fraction of an inch will work, but they should not touch. Air-fry undisturbed for 10 minutes, or until golden brown and crisp.
5. Gently dump the contents of the basket onto a wire rack. Cool for at least 5 minutes or up to 15 minutes before serving.

Pineapple Sticks

Servings: 4
Cooking Time: 20 Minutes
Ingredients:
- ½ fresh pineapple, cut into sticks
- ¼ cup desiccated coconut

Directions:
1. Pre-heat the Air Fryer to 400°F (205°C).
2. Coat the pineapple sticks in the desiccated coconut and put each one in the Air Fryer basket.
3. Air fry for 10 minutes.

Nutella And Banana Pastries

Servings:4
Cooking Time:12 Minutes
Ingredients:
- 1 puff pastry sheet, cut into 4 equal squares
- ½ cup Nutella
- 2 bananas, sliced
- 2 tablespoons icing sugar

Directions:
1. Preheat the Air fryer to 375°F (1905°C) and grease an Air fryer basket.
2. Spread Nutella on each pastry square and top with banana slices and icing sugar.
3. Fold each square into a triangle and slightly press the edges with a fork.
4. Arrange the pastries in the Air fryer basket and cook for about 12 minutes.
5. Dish out and serve immediately.

Ninja Air Fryer Cookbook

Recipes Index

15-minute Chicken 69

A
Ahi Tuna Steaks 59
Air Fried Calamari 53
Air Fried Grilled Steak 79
Air Fried Thyme Garlic Lamb Chops 72
All-in-one Breakfast Toast 40
Almond Topped Trout 52
Amazing Blooming Onion 26
Apple Pie 85
Apple Rollups 23
Asparagus Fries 12
Asparagus Wrapped In Pancetta 12

B
Bacon & Blue Cheese Tartlets 23
Bacon And Blue Cheese Burgers 72
Bacon And Cheese Quiche 30
Bacon And Cheese–stuffed Pork Chops 76
Bacon Chicken Mix 65
Bacon Eggs 30
Bacon Puff Pastry Pinwheels 33
Bacon, Egg, And Cheese Calzones 38
Bacon-jalapeño Cheesy "breadsticks" 15
Bacon-wrapped Asparagus 15
Bacon-wrapped Cabbage Bites 26
Bacon-wrapped Goat Cheese Poppers 26
Bacon-wrapped Jalapeño Poppers 23
Bagels 31
Baked Apple 88
Baked Jalapeño And Cheese Cauliflower Mash 13
Banana And Rice Pudding 86
Banana Baked Oatmeal 37
Banana Chips With Chocolate Glaze 88
Banana-nut Muffins 39
Barbecue Chicken Enchiladas 66
Barbecue Country-style Pork Ribs 75
Basic Chicken Breasts 63
Basil Pork Bites 21
Basil Tomatoes 49
Beer-battered Cod 57
Black's Bangin' Casserole 28
Blackened Chicken Tenders 67
Blackened Steak Nuggets 82
Blistered Tomatoes 15
Blueberry Muffins 31
Blueberry Scones 29
Boneless Ribeyes 78
Breadcrumbs Stuffed Mushrooms 45
Breaded Chicken Patties 69
Breakfast Chimichangas 31

Breakfast Quiche 38
Brown Sugar Cookies 88
Brown Sugar Mustard Pork Loin 71
Brussels Sprouts 17
Buffalo Chicken Meatballs 67
Bunless Breakfast Turkey Burgers 34
Buttered Broccoli 44
Buttered Brussels Sprouts 18
Buttermilk Biscuits 17
Buttermilk-fried Chicken Thighs 68
Buttery Scallops 36

C
Cajun Flounder Fillets 53
Cajun Lobster Tails 54
Cajun Salmon 58
Caprese Eggplant Stacks 42
Caramelized Brussels Sprout 46
Caraway Seed Pretzel Sticks 19
Catalan Sardines With Romesco Sauce 60
Catfish Nuggets 56
Cauliflower Buns 24
Cauliflower Pizza Crust 43
Cauliflower Rice–stuffed Peppers 43
Cauliflower Steaks Gratin 48
Celery Chicken Mix 65
Cheddar Bacon Ranch Pinwheels 76
Cheddar Cheese Lumpia Rolls 22
Cheese And Bean Enchiladas 49
Cheese Pie 30
Cheesy Baked Asparagus 17
Cheesy Cauliflower "hash Browns" 35
Cheesy Garlic Bread 17
Cheesy Tortellini Bites 25
Chicken Fajita Poppers 65
Chicken Fried Steak 82
Chicken Nuggets 66
Chicken Parmesan Casserole 65
Chicken Sausage In Dijon Sauce 63
Chicken Wings 64
Chicken Wrapped In Bacon 64
Chili-lime Shrimp 55
Chives Omelet 32
Chocolate Chip Cookie Cake 87
Chocolate Chip Muffins 31
Chocolate Chip Scones 29
Chocolate-hazelnut Bear Claws 29
Cinnamon Apple Crisps 22
Cinnamon Canned Biscuit Donuts 89
Cinnamon Granola 36
Cinnamon Pretzels 84
Cinnamon Rolls 28
Cinnamon-sugar Pretzel Bites 84

Cocoa Bombs 84
Cod Nuggets 54
Crab-stuffed Avocado Boats 59
Cream Cheese Danish 36
Creamy Parsley Soufflé 33
Crème Brulee 85
Crispy 'n Salted Chicken Meatballs 69
Crispy "fried" Chicken 62
Crispy Bacon 28
Crispy Cabbage Steaks 44
Crispy Eggplant Rounds 50
Crispy Ham And Eggs 79
Crispy Herbed Potatoes 17
Crispy Italian Chicken Thighs 65
Crispy Shawarma Broccoli 44
Crispy Smoked Pork Chops 75
Crispy Wings With Lemony Old Bay Spice 44
Crunchy And Buttery Cod With Ritz Cracker Crust 58
Crunchy Coconut Shrimp 52
Curried Eggplant 50
Custard 85

D

Dauphinoise (potatoes Au Gratin) 14
Dill Pickle–ranch Wings 67

E

Easy & Crispy Chicken Wings 68
Easy & The Traditional Beef Roast Recipe 74
Easy Baked Root Veggies 47
Easy Egg Bites 37
Easy Glazed Carrots 44
Easy Keto Danish 87
Easy Lobster Tail With Salted Butetr 59
Easy Parmesan Asparagus 15
Easy-peasy Beef Sliders 76
Easy-peasy Shrimp 60
Egg In A Hole 28
Egg Muffins 32
Egg Stuffed Pork Meatballs 71
Egg White Cups 37
Egg White Frittata 35
Eggplant Parmesan Subs 36
Eggplant Parmesan 47
Eggs In Avocado Halves 25
Empanadas 75

F

Fajita Flank Steak Rolls 77
Fiesta Pastries 85
Fish Fillet Sandwich 53
Fish Sticks 56
Flatbread Dippers 19
Flatiron Steak Grill On Parsley Salad 73
Flounder Fillets 55
Foil Packet Lemon Butter Asparagus 13
Fried Banana S'mores 89
Fried Goat Cheese 22
Fried Herbed Chicken Wings 63
Fried Mashed Potato Balls 13
Fried Pineapple Chunks 89
Fried Ranch Pickles 26
Fry Bread 31

G

Garlic And Dill Salmon 60
Garlic And Oregano Lamb Chops 81
Garlic Breadsticks 21
Garlic Dill Wings 63
Garlic Fillets 73
Garlic Ginger Chicken 66
Garlic Okra Chips 44
Garlic Parmesan Drumsticks 62
Glazed Donuts 88
Greek Pork Chops 80
Green Beans 13
Green Peas With Mint 12
Green Scramble 32
Grilled Bbq Sausages 34
Grilled Cheese Sandwich Deluxe 22
Grilled Steak With Parsley Salad 38

H

Hasselback Alfredo Chicken 63
Healthy Apple-licious Chips 46
Hearty Banana Pastry 88
Herbed Haddock 56
Herb-marinated Chicken 63
Hole In One 32
Home-style Taro Chips 21
Honey Mesquite Pork Chops 72
Honey Tater Tots With Bacon 21
Horseradish-crusted Salmon Fillets 56
Hot Coconut 'n Cocoa Buns 85
Hot Okra Wedges 16

I

Inside-out Cheeseburgers 39
Italian Baked Cod 57
Italian Chicken Thighs 64
Italian Roasted Chicken Thighs 67
Italian Seasoned Easy Pasta Chips 42

J

Jalapeño And Bacon Breakfast Pizza 36
Jalapeño Egg Cups 33

K

Kiwi Pastry Bites 86

L

Lamb Burgers 82
Lamb Chops 80
Lemon Butter–dill Salmon 55
Lemon Caper Cauliflower Steaks 49

Lemon Pepper Chicken Wings 64
Lemon Pepper–breaded Tilapia 55
Lemon Shrimp And Zucchinis 55
Lemon Tofu Cubes 24
Lemon-butter Veal Cutlets 73
Lemon-roasted Salmon Fillets 57
Lime Bay Scallops 60
Lobster Tails 52
London Broil 80

M

Maple Butter Salmon 52
Maple'n Soy Marinated Beef 79
Marinated Steak Kebabs 82
Marshmallow Pastries 87
Mccornick Pork Chops 79
Meaty Omelet 30
Mediterranean Egg Sandwich 30
Mediterranean Pan Pizza 48
Medium Rare Simple Salt And Pepper Steak 34
Mexican Muffins 25
Mexican-style Shredded Beef 72
Mini Bacon Egg Quiches 32
Mini Hasselback Potatoes 16
Mini Tomato Quiche 37
Miso-rubbed Salmon Fillets 57
Molten Lava Cakes 86
Mouth-watering Provençal Mushrooms 15
Mozzarella-stuffed Meatloaf 74
Mustard Herb Pork Tenderloin 74
Mustard Pork 80

N

Nutella And Banana Pastries 89
Nutty Fudge Muffins 87

O

Okra Chips 23
Onion Marinated Skirt Steak 29
Orange And Brown Sugar–glazed Ham 77
Orange Marmalade 84
Oregano And Coconut Scramble 30
Oreo-coated Peanut Butter Cups 86
Outrageous Crispy Fried Salmon Skin 56

P

Pancake For Two 39
Pancetta Mushroom & Onion Sautée 16
Panko-breaded Cod Fillets 54
Paprika Duck 64
Parmesan Garlic Naan 38
Parmesan-crusted Pork Chops 73
Parsley Omelet 34
Party Buffalo Chicken Drumettes 68
Pecan-crusted Chicken Tenders 62
Peppered Steak Bites 71
Pepper-pineapple With Butter-sugar Glaze 46
Peppery Lemon-chicken Breast 65

Perfect Broccoli 16
Perfect Burgers 33
Perfect French Fries 14
Pesto Vegetable Kebabs 42
Pesto-rubbed Veal Chops 79
Pickled Chips 21
Pigs In A Blanket 34
Pineapple Sticks 89
Pizza Dough 42
Pizza Eggs 39
Polenta 14
Pork Belly Marinated In Onion-coconut Cream 74
Pork Chops 77
Pork Spare Ribs 81
Potato-wrapped Salmon Fillets 59

Q

Quick & Easy Meatballs 72
Quick & Simple Bratwurst With Vegetables 78
Quick 'n Easy Garlic Herb Wings 67

R

Rib Eye Steak Seasoned With Italian Herb 78
Rib Eye Steak 71
Roast Beef 81
Roasted Brussels Sprouts With Bacon 12
Roasted Chickpeas 25
Roasted Fennel Salad 14
Roasted Garlic And Thyme Tomatoes 18
Roasted Garlic 13
Roasted Golden Mini Potatoes 37
Roasted Peppers 22
Roasted Rhubarb 14
Roasted Vegetable Pita Pizza 47
Root Vegetable Crisps 24
Rosemary Lamb Chops 79
Rosemary Partridge 68
Rumaki 21

S

S'mores Pockets 85
Salmon Patties 58
Salt And Pepper Wings 66
Salted 'n Peppered Scored Beef Chuck 76
Sautéed Spinach 46
Sea Salt Radishes 15
Sesame Tuna Steak 52
Shrimp Al Pesto 58
Simple Egg Soufflé 34
Simple Lamb Chops 80
Simple Roasted Sweet Potatoes 14
Simple Salmon Fillets 59
Simple Salmon 60
Smashed Fried Baby Potatoes 12
Smoked Salmon Croissant Sandwich 35
Smokehouse-style Beef Ribs 77
Snow Crab Legs 53
Southern-style Catfish 53

Spice-rubbed Chicken Thighs	68
Spice-rubbed Pork Loin	74
Spicy Corn Fritters	19
Spicy Fish Taco Bowl	54
Spicy Fried Green Beans	18
Spicy Roasted Cashew Nuts	46
Spinach 'n Bacon Egg Cups	65
Spinach And Artichoke–stuffed Peppers	43
Spinach And Feta Pinwheels	48
Spinach And Feta Stuffed Chicken Breasts	62
Spinach And Mushroom Steak Rolls	81
Spinach And Provolone Steak Rolls	78
Spinach Pesto Flatbread	42
Spinach Spread	35
Spinach-bacon Rollups	29
Steak Bites And Spicy Dipping Sauce	80
Steak Fingers	74
Steakhouse Filets Mignons	78
Sticky Drumsticks	69
Strawberry Pastry	35
Strawberry Shortcake	84
Stuffed Chicken	64
Stuffed Peppers	77
Stuffed Portobellos	46
Sweet And Sour Brussel Sprouts	45
Sweet And Spicy Barbecue Tofu	45
Sweet And Spicy Pork Ribs	75
Sweet And Spicy Spare Ribs	73
Sweet Apple Fries	24
Sweet Pepper Nachos	46
Sweet Potato-cinnamon Toast	38
Sweet Potato–wrapped Shrimp	60

T

Taco Okra	18
Tacos	45
Tasty Brussels Sprouts With Guanciale	18
Teriyaki Chicken Kebabs	67
Thai Turkey Sausage Patties	33

Thyme Lentil Patties	45
Thyme Scallops	55
Thyme Sweet Potato Chips	24
Tilapia Fish Fillets	53
Tilapia Teriyaki	54
Timeless Garlic-lemon Scallops	52
Tortilla Fried Pies	88
Tortilla Pizza Margherita	42
Tortilla-crusted With Lemon Filets	58
Tuna And Arugula Salad	28
Tuna-stuffed Tomatoes	58
Turmeric Crispy Chickpeas	48
Twice-baked Broccoli-cheddar Potatoes	49
Twice-baked Potatoes With Pancetta	16
Two-cheese Grilled Sandwiches	48

V

Veggie Chips	23
Venison Backstrap	76
Very Berry Breakfast Puffs	28

W

Wasabi-coated Pork Loin Chops	71
White Cheddar And Mushroom Soufflés	43
White Wheat Walnut Bread	39
Wine Infused Mushrooms	49

Y

Yummy Shredded Chicken	66
Yummy Stuffed Chicken Breast	66

Z

Za'atar Garbanzo Beans	25
Zesty Mahi Mahi	59
Zesty Ranch Chicken Drumsticks	69
Zucchini And Spring Onions Cakes	37
Zucchini Gratin	43
Zucchini Topped With Coconut Cream 'n Bacon	47

Printed in Great Britain
by Amazon